THE
B*WITCHED
STORY

Pippa Richardson

B⬡XTREE

First published 1999 by Boxtree
an imprint of Macmillan Publishers Ltd
25 Eccleston Place London SW1W 9NF
Basingstoke and Oxford

www.macmillan.co.uk

Associated companies throughout the world

ISBN 0 7522 1822 0

1 3 5 7 9 8 6 4 2

A CIP catalogue record for this book
is available from the British Library.

Typeset by SX Composing DTP, Rayleigh, Essex
Printed by Mackays of Chatham PLC, Chatham, Kent

THE
B*WITCHED
STORY

Also available:

The STEPS Story by Teresa Maughan

Contents

CHAPTER ONE

The Spell is Cast . . .

If ever there was a day when magic was at work – if ever there was a time when the forces of the universe were at work to create something, well, bewitching – it was probably a day in 1996 when a lady called Mrs O'Carroll decided to have her car fixed in a garage in Dublin.

On the surface of it, it was a very boring day. Mrs O'Carroll's car needed a bit of work doing to it so she drove it to a garage in the city owned by a Mr Brendan Lynch and, as far as she was concerned, that was that. Yet unbeknown to her, her daughter, Sinead, got chatting to a mechanic in the garage, unleashing a spell which would change the face of pop music. And the mechanic? Well, she (yup, she) was Mr Lynch's daughter, a slip of a girl called Keavy who was working part time for her Da as a tyre changer. And that conversation, between Keavy Lynch and Sinead O'Carroll, sparked the beginnings of a band that have gone on to rule the world's pop charts. It was the beginning of B*Witched.

To be fair, Sinead, Keavy and their fellow band members Lindsay Armaou and Edele Lynch (Keavy's twin sister) had seen each other before. All four of them attended dance classes at Dublin's famous Digges Lane dance studio (where the likes of Boyzone and OTT had trained before them). But they only knew each other to say hello to and that was it. After that day in the garage, however, the four of them came together in a way which was to change their lives.

'It was just one of those thing,' Keavy said later. 'I started talking to Sinead while I changed a wheel on a car and we got talking and realised we had a lot in common.' What they had in common was a desire to be in a band. At the same time, Keavy had met Lindsay at kick-boxing classes and already knew that she was interested in forming some sort of pop group, so within hours of meeting Sinead she organised for the four girls to meet up.

As soon as they met, the girls realised they had something special, and virtually the very next day they booked time in a studio at Digges Lane to work together on songs and choreography.

'We just clicked,' Edele says now. 'Even on our first day in the studio we knew.'

At the time, Lindsay was the only one of the four still at school. Keavy was working at the garage, her sister Edele was working in a sports shop and Sinead, the only one of the four who had any professional performing experience, was working at a theatre in Dublin. Sinead takes up the story . . .

'We all had day jobs at the time,' she recalls, 'all apart from Lindsay – but we'd come to the studio for three hours a night. People would be like, 'What are you doing?' and we'd reply, 'We're training for our dreams.'

*

About two weeks later, another ingredient was added to the spell – this time a piece of luck which is the weirdest coincidence known to man. One day, as the girls were rehearsing at Digges Lane, a TV crew from the Irish national television station RTE turned up to make a documentary about the studio and spotted the girls working together. There and then they asked the quartet to perform on the station's Saturday morning show, THAT WEEKEND.

The TV moguls realised that the future B*Witched had something no other band had.

'When we first got famous people called us the Irish Spice Girls but weren't really influenced by them,' Sinead says now. 'When we were getting ourselves together they were just coming out as well – in fact I think we were together before they came out.'

'We just wanted to be something different,' says Edele. 'We knew something different had to be done, something that hadn't been done before, and I think Irish music is quite different.'

Unfortunately, at the time the girls were asked to appear on TV, they hadn't had time to record a song (they had been practising singing without music!) so they got what little money they had together and hurriedly went into a studio to lay down a track.

What they came up with was three songs – 'A Shoulder to Cry on', 'True Love' and a ditty called 'Ain't Nobody Crying'. That done, they had to quickly come up with a name, and they chose D'Zire because, as Lindsay recalls, they were getting 'what we desired'!

Obviously, the four girls were extremely nervous about their debut TV performance, and spent every possible moment perfecting their routines. Then there was the question of what to wear. Unlike most professional pop groups, they didn't have a stylist, so the four had to go out shopping to put together their outfits – which ended up being quite tomboyish. The most extravagant thing they bought were boots that cost £120 each – a week of Keavy's wages!

'We spent a lot of money in the beginning,' Sinead said later, remembering the spree. 'But it's all paid off now!'

It certainly did pay off. On the strength of the TV show, D'Zire were asked to support Boyzone on tour – which led to the final magical happening in the B*Witched spell . . .

During their first live show, at Belfast's Kings Hall, the four girls were spotted by a lady in the audience who goes by the name of Kim Glover. Kim, it turned out, was a band manager – she had once managed the huge US teen band New Kids On The Block – and, despite the fact that the lights didn't go on during the girls' first song, she was mightily impressed by what she saw.

'There was just a magical quality about them,' Kim told *The Times* later. 'They sang fantastically well, they moved well, they were just fantastic girls. Then when I found out they could write songs too, that was just fantastic. They're the genuine article.'

Kim arranged to meet the girls later, in a hotel in Dublin, and having got to know them better, agreed to manage their careers. Her first move was to get them together with the famous Irish producer Ray Hedges (who had written and crafted records for Ant and Dec and Boyzone) to see if he would help them put some tunes together.

Ray and Kim decided that D'Zire, as they were then, needed some more experience of performing and so, when they weren't in the studio recording, the girls went on a four-month tour of schools, singing and dancing for an audience of very critical record-buyers!

The next thing the girls had to deal with was their name. They'd chosen the name D'Zire in a hurry and, on reflection, neither they nor Kim were happy with it, so they changed it to Sassy. They'd just got used to this when – wouldn't you know it! – they discovered that another band had the same name, so their monicker was changed for a second time, this time to Sister. It was a name, but it wasn't a great name – and luckily for them Ray Hedges had a bit of a brainwave . . .

'B*Witched actually came from Ray,' Sinead recalled later. 'At first he didn't want to work with a girl band because he thought there were too many of us out there. But our Kim and her partner Tom asked him to hear us sing and when we sang to him he said we bewitched him. So we decided on Bewitched.'

All it took then was for the addition of the star instead of the 'e' in the name (a ploy thought up by Keavy and Edele's brother Shane of Boyzone – see Chapter Six!) and B*Witched were set well on their way.

There was, however, the small matter of a recording contract – i.e. they didn't have one yet. While the girls were working hard at perfecting their singing and dancing, Kim and Ray had arranged for them to meet with various record company bosses. One happened to be a certain Rob Stringer, MD of Epic records. He was quite taken by the girls, and gave them a 'development deal' – nine months in which to develop their sound and come up with songs for an album. Nine months seemed like a very long time, but it flew by as the girls worked on songwriting and producing a sound they were happy with. The first songs they and Ray came up with were 'C'est La Vie' and 'To You I Belong'. Not bad for starters!

Just as the development deal was ending, the girls were enjoying a quick bite to eat in a café when they got the telephone call through to say that Epic definitely wanted to release their album. Not surprisingly, they all burst out crying with happiness.

'I think getting signed was down to our drive and ambition,' Sinead says now, looking back. 'We were determined to succeed and weren't afraid to work hard to get it.'

And so, abracadabra, B*Witched was born.

Within months of signing their deal, the foursome were doing all sorts of interviews with papers and magazines that had heard about the new band and were eager to feature them in their pages. One of the first B*Witched interviews was with the *Daily Star*.

'We're not just another girl band,' Keavy told the reporter. 'We're B*Witched, and once you see us you'll be under our spell.'

How right she was.

CHAPTER TWO

Lindsay Gael Christina Elaine Armaou

Nickname: Linds
Birth date: 18 December 1980
Born: Athens, Greece
Star sign: Sagittarius

When Lindsay Armaou was thirteen, her entire life changed in the space of twelve months. She began the year as an ordinary schoolgirl who spoke Greek and had lived in Athens her entire life. The year ended with Linds living in Ireland, thousand of miles away from her friends and very, very cold.

Lindsay, who was born in Greece, had lived there with her mum Sharon (who is from Ireland) and her Greek dad Iannis (who owns a hotel) since she was born. Unfortunately, in the year she became a teenager, her mum split from her dad and moved to Ireland – taking Linds, her only child, with her.

'My life totally changed,' she says now. 'When my mum

first told me we were moving I was shocked and scared but I got used to the idea and began to get excited.'

'I suppose the hardest thing was having to leave my dad,' she recalls. 'My parents had separated and he stayed in Greece, but we kept in touch and I'm always going out to visit him.'

When Lindsay first arrived in Dublin she was quite depressed. She was away from her three best friends (though, luckily, they have still managed to keep in touch over the years) and found herself feeling the lowest she ever had. It turned out that she suffered quite badly from Seasonal Affective Disorder – a condition in which people get depressed when they haven't had enough sun – and Lindsay was desperate to get back to a warmer country.

'It did get cold in Greece,' she remembers, 'but it very rarely rained and never snowed like it did in Ireland.'

Luckily she eventually managed to settle in Ireland (thoroughly enjoying her first ever snowball fight that same year!) and now considers herself to be Irish through and through.

'I'm lucky in that I'm quite adaptable and outgoing, so deep down I knew I'd be okay,' she smiles. 'I don't regret having to move from Greece. Everything happens for a reason and, let's face it, if I hadn't moved here B*Witched never would have happened.'

Lindsay soon got lots of new friends in Ireland and became a popular fixture at her new school. She was a bit of a whizz when it came to extra-curricular activities. She joined the school choir and orchestra (in which she played piano and guitar) and even took part in some of the school's musicals (she played one of the brothers in *Joseph and the Amazing Technicolor Dreamcoat!*). In fact, Lindsay's first brush with fame came from one particular outing she had with her school choir.

'The choir was in the local paper when we won a competition,' she grins. If only she'd known that this recognition of her musical talent would be the first of many newspaper and magazine cuttings she'd be amassing throughout her life!

While Lindsay was having all this fun, and developing her great Irish accent, she also became quite academic – a real A student.

'I was very bright and diligent at school,' she says honestly. 'I always did very well.' She was popular with the teachers as well as the pupils and rarely got a homework assignment that she couldn't complete with top marks.

But despite her academic success, deep inside our Lindsay always knew that she wanted to be a pop star. It was this dream which drove her to attend dancing classes at the Digges Lane studios – and the spur which helped fate get her together with Edele, Keavy and Sinead. Lindsay reckons that from day one she knew that the four of them working together felt 'right'. It was obvious to her from the beginning that somewhere along the line the four girls would mange to create something special, although quite what that something special would be she couldn't even imagine.

Yet, sensible as ever, Lindsay continued with her studying. She did brilliantly in her Irish School Leaving Certificate exams (getting 460 points out of a total of 600) and right up until B*Witched signed a deal with Epic records she was planning to go to Trinity College in Dublin to study for a Business degree.

'But look, I always wanted to be a pop star,' she grins now. 'I had a place to go to college and study business, but when we got the recording contract I said, "No, I'm going to go for it." And I'm well glad that I did.'

The other B*Witched girls make no secret of the fact that Lindsay is the most popular 'witcher with the lads, which Linds puts down to her flirtiness.

She also has piles and piles of energy. When asked to describe herself, Lindsay has no hesitation in pointing out what an active B*Witcher she really is.

'I'm bubbly, ambitious, giggly, friendly and laid back,' she says. 'And I hate getting up and going to bed. I hate sleeping, full stop!'

But while she has a great zest for life, Lindsay also manages to be the calmest member of B*Witched. She finds it very easy to kick back her heels and chill out, no matter how much pressure the hectic B*Witched schedules put on her and her three buddies.

'Lindsay's very laid back,' says Edele. 'She's got a calm vibe to her.'

Lindsay agrees. 'The thing I miss most about life before B*Witched is having time to veg out,' she laughs. It'll be a long time before she has any more of that!

Fame has changed Lindsay's life in ways she could never have imagined. 'I can't seem to go anywhere without someone recognising me,' she laughs. ' But I'm not complaining – we are very lucky to do what we are doing.'

And being well known obviously does have its advantages.

'I went to a Chinese restaurant and the staff asked for my autograph,' she recalls. 'When it was time to pay the bill they just ripped it up!' Nice work if you can get it . . .

Yet, to Lindsay, fame will never be the best part of being in B*Witched. She appreciates her friendship with the girls, and loves the fact that the band's music touches their fans.

'It's not about fame,' she says. 'I know it sounds corny but it's not. It's about being successful. If one fan writes to me and says I was in a bad depressed state and I listened to your album and it made me feel better, then I'm successful.'

B*witching facts about Lindsay . . .

* Lindsay reckons her eyes change colour, depending on what kind of mood she's in. 'They go from green to orange to brown,' she claims.

* She's the only member of B*Witched who can 'twinkle' her nose like the character Samantha on the sixties American TV show *Bewitched*.

* When Lindsay was ten she saved a litter of kittens from drowning in a river.

* When she first joined B*Witched (then called Sassy) Lindsay bleached her hair blonde and had it cut short! Before that she had long wavy locks which she was really proud of. 'When I had it cut from long to short my hairdresser got carried away,' she laughed. 'I looked like a boy!'

* She's extremely fearful of sharks. 'They're really scary!'
* The first record she ever bought was 'Bad!' by Michael Jackson.
* Even though she was the only member of B*Witched who was still at school when B*Witched met, she did have a temporary job as a shop assistant at a place called Julien's in Dublin's St Stephens Street.
* Her favourite food is fruit 'like mangoes, bananas and watermelons'.
* She reckons she has a hidden talent for dress designing and, er, eyebrow shaping.
* She collects teddies. 'But I haven't so many as Edele, though. She got millions of them!'
* She is most likely to say, 'Are you serious?! Oh really?'
* Her motto is, 'A dream can become reality if you work at it.'

CHAPTER THREE

Edele Edwina Christina Lynch

Nickname: Eddie
Birth date: 15 December 1979
Born: Dublin, Ireland
Star sign: Sagittarius

It's easy to tell the difference between Edele Lynch and her sister – well, easy if you know how. And it's all thanks to a game she played with Keavy on their third birthday.

The pair were messing about in the living room of their house in Dublin, pretending to be aeroplanes (as you do), when Edele tripped and fell against the concrete step of their fireplace. Unluckily for her, she knocked the top of her nose really badly. She was rushed to hospital and had to have eighteen stitches, leaving a perfect scar on the bridge of her nose. Apparently, while Edele was having the stitches, Keavy was staying with her Auntie Ann and cried from the moment Edele went into the operating theatre until the moment she came out, saying she had a really bad headache!

'It was quite weird actually,' says Edele. 'We looked different for a bit – and then Keavy's eyebrows grew across right after, so we looked the same – she had the eyebrows and I had the scar.'

Sisterly love, huh?

Despite their identical twin-ness, Edele is definitely the more forthright of the sisters.

'I'm a perfectionist – try to be anyway. People call me the leader 'cause I'm quite confident and I always keep my secrets to myself,' she says. 'I'm the level-headed one. I'm more focused – the boss sister. When we were growing up Keavy would look to me for decisions.'

Keavy agrees.

'Edele's quite a lot stronger than me,' she says, musing. 'I think it takes more to make her cry so it seems worse when she does. She's very good at putting up a front . . . actually a lot of people say Edele looks older than me, but I'm twenty minutes older!

'Edele's is a very strong person,' she continues. 'We all go to Edele 'cause she knows how to talk to people and how to handle everybody. She knows how to say things.'

Growing up, Edele's favourite subjects at school were art and metalwork (she was the only girl in the metalwork class which, she says, was quite 'embarrassing'!) and she did have brief dreams, at one time, of being a gymnast, but those thoughts died out when she hurt her knee at the age of thirteen. It was a blessing in disguise, as she then con-centrated on her first love – performing.

To begin with, dancing was her thing. She started going

to ballet classes after school (imagine her in her tutu doing fairy dances!) and then went on to take jazz dance classes with her elder sister, Tara. Later on, Edele, Tara, Keavy and a friend of theirs, Pamela, formed their own disco dancing team called Starlight (for which their very patient 'Supermum' Mrs Lynch made all the costumes!) and had a riot making up dance routines and taking part in competitions. At about the same time, Edele started singing with Keaves, and they were so good they even went on to win a karaoke competition at a holiday camp when they were in their early teens.

'I don't think there was any moment when I just knew I wanted to be famous,' Edele recalls. 'Saying that, I remember when Keavy and myself where growing up we always wanted to sing and dance. I do remember I was in the car one day when I was twelve or thirteen and I was singing "Eternal Flame" by the Bangles (which is my favourite song) and my Mam turned around and said, "Ah, you sing that beautifully, Edele." From that day, I said to myself I was going to do it, long before Shane was in a band.

'You know what it's like. When you're young and you say you want to be a pop star people say, "Ah, don't be silly, what's the real job you want to do? To be in a pop group you have to be beautiful and people have to look up to you . . . " But my mother and father were behind us all the way.'

Edele's musical talents didn't just lie in her singing voice; she turned out to be a mean flute player too. And to make some money when the girls were in their teens, Edele and Keavy decided to use their boogying talents teaching dance classes. Edele also worked, for a time, in Stadium Sports in

Dublin – just to make a bit of cash to pay for her dance lessons. If only she and her sis had known then that they were going to become huge pop stars . . .

'I love what we do,' Edele laughs enthusiastically. 'The energy is the most important thing. It's about having fun.' This from the girl who wrote 'lots of giggles' on this year's B*Witched Christmas card!

'It's a great job,' she continues. 'Being spotted or being asked for an autograph is so exciting. Some people scream at us like you'd never believe. Even when people just say, "Who are you? Are you famous?" it spins me out. We've been waiting a long time for this.'

And she intends to enjoy every minute of it. 'We're living a dream,' she smiles, 'and we don't want to wish our time away.'

In fact, she says, the only thing she misses at all about her life before fame is her mammy's cooking.

'It's deadly!'

B*Witching stuff about Edele . . .

* Edele's favourite food is seafood, especially lobster. 'If I see or smell lobster I just have to have some,' she told a journalist. 'You could say I'm lobster mad.'
* Despite having had a hit single with 'Rollercoaster', Edele is scared witless of the things.
* She's desperately superstitious, and won't go anywhere without her lucky teddy Patch, which her parents bought for her before the band's first showcase.

* She reckons she once broke the ceiling in her house . . . because she couldn't get her hair right. 'I was getting ready to go to a party and I was trying to fix my hair while standing on the upstairs landing,' she tells us. 'It wouldn't go right, so I started to jump up and down in frustration. Then I heard a crash and the light had fallen out of the ceiling downstairs.'

* The first record she bought was 'Billie Jean' by Michael Jackson.

* She's a bit potty about the colour yellow – even her ice cream has to be yellow. Not white . . . YELLOW!

* She's scared of spiders . . . and rollercoasters!

* She likes water-skiing and used to play basketball before B*Witched took up most of her time!

* Her most used phrase is, 'That drives me mad!'

* When she gets time off she likes to stay home in her pyjamas and sit in front of the telly catching up on her favourite TV programmes.

* Her motto? 'Don't listen to people telling you you can't do it; once you believe, you can do it yourself.'

CHAPTER FOUR

Keavy Jane Elizabeth Annie Lynch

Nickname: Keaves
Birth date: 15 December 1979
Born: Dublin, Ireland
Star sign: Sagittarius

She describes herself as 'shy, laid back, cute, giddy and happy' – and no one could put it better. Keavy Lynch is the life and soul of B*Witched: she's cute, she's funny and possibly the most positive person you could ever meet. That's if she knows what to say to you . . . 'cause if she's in the wrong frame of mind our Keaves can be as shy as a mouse.

'I've always been a bit shyer than Edele,' she grins. 'I never know what to say to new people! Everybody says I'm cute and giddy. You just have to look at me and laugh . . . '

That's not to say she hasn't got a naughty streak. She and Edele got into a canny few scrapes when they were young. Like the incident in which they managed to blow up their mammy's car ('She had this gorgeous white car and we sat in the back of it and found some matches,' she laughs. 'Edele took one out of the box and I said, "Go on, strike it." I was egging her on . . .') or the time that she and Keavy were found, er, eating coal.

'It's the earliest thing I remember,' she says, 'me and Edele sitting in the coal bunker eating coal. We were still in nappies – I think we were about two. My mum and dad thought it was funny, took a picture of us and then said, "Get out of there".'

Yet despite her scrapes, Keavy has always managed to come across as the perfect angel, which is probably why, when she and Edele were still in nappies, they managed to win first prize in a bonny baby competition (their first award!). It's probably also why, when Keavy was still only seven, she was picked to appear in a calendar to publicise a holiday camp. The pic showed her sitting on a small train, waving . . .

'All my life I've had a brilliant time,' she laughs. 'We did so many fun things. But it was always to keep us out of trouble . . .

'Some of the best times were our summer holidays in Donabate where we had a caravan. We'd go there for two or three weeks ever year. There was our family and the Couteneys, who are a big family – they have five kids – and all the kids would hang out together. We'd come in for lunch and there'd be all these stilts and skateboards and bikes flung everywhere.'

It was apparent from very early on that Keavy was going to be a star. Even when she and Edele were wee little things, the pair were always desperate to perform. According to Keavy, singing and dancing were just hobbies for her and her twin sis. 'It made us happy,' she cackles.

'Every year we'd get together with some cousins who lived around the corner and prepare a little show,' she says now. 'Edele and I made up all these songs for it and everybody would do their talents. My granddad plays the fiddle and we'd always sing and dance.'

Despite the dream of being a famous pop star, as Keavy grew up she developed more down-to-earth interests – probably because she's always been a terrible tomboy.

At school, her favourite subject was PE; she was so good at it that she managed to win medals for gymnastics and swimming. What an athlete! What's more, when Keavy was seventeen, she developed a bit of a penchant for kick-boxing! She became so good at it that even now she holds a blue belt and would love to study some more – if she ever gets the time. Her kick-boxing skills were highly developed and, for a while there, her instructor, Martin, wanted her to take part in competitions. But Keavy refused: it turns out that she doesn't agree with people getting into a kick-boxing ring and hurting each other. (Still, must remember never to cross her . . . !)

As well as being fierce with her martial arts, our timid ickle Keavy was also loyal at school and was known as being a good friend to have – a trait she's proud of to this day.

'Once everyone in my class fell out with one of my mates, and I stayed her best friend no matter what everyone else said,' she says proudly. So, as you can see, our Keaves may be shy, but she knows the difference between right and wrong, and she'll stick by her principles to the end.

She's a grounded chick and, when she was younger, she had pretty down-to-earth career ambitions too. For a brief period of time she fancied being a firewoman, but then became fascinated by her dad's garage business – which was how she ended up working as a trainee mechanic.

'It sounds really weird to say I was a mechanic, but that's because my dad owns a garage and I always wanted to know a bit more about cars. I worked there for about a year and a half.

'I always wanted to know more about cars than just the fact you drive around in them. That's the main difference between me and Edele. She's not into cars. In fact, she's scared of them.'

Of course, Keavy has spent all of her life with her best mate and twin sister Edele, and no matter what she's done in her life or where she's been, she's always had to maintain a close contact with her sis. She clearly remembers the first time that she and Edele were parted: it was when was when they got their first jobs, working in the same sports shop . . . and she was sent to a different branch.

'It was so strange,' she says. 'We kind of got used to it but I rang her every hour just to say hello.'

Like Edele, Keavy was always a dance fanatic, and it was her older sister Tara who suggested that she go to the Digges Lane dance studio in Dublin to take jazz dancing classes. On her first ever day of lessons she was actually late because she didn't want to turn up without the proper shoes and trousers, so she made her mum and dad run around town with her to buy some before the lesson began. As it happened, when she got there she was the only one with the right uniform anyway!

As well as the disco dancing thing that they both got into (see Edele's profile), Keavy and her sis also began to do hip-hop and formed a group called Boom with their friends Danny, Mark, Pagan and Graham. As if that wasn't enough, Keavy also joined a marching band called the Dublin All Stars in which she played the saxophone and paraded around twirling a flag. She certainly packed a lot into her life before B*Witched!

Ask Edele how she'd describe Keavy and she says, 'She's funny, and a bit quiet,' but we think she's joking about the quiet part! The truth is that if there's a trick to be played in B*Witched or a joke to be told, Keavy is probably behind it. She's also a bit clumsy – hence the time that she knocked over a mirror in Amsterdam and snapped it in half. Luckily, B*Witched don't believe in seven years' bad luck.

Today Keavy wouldn't change a thing about her pop star existence. Despite her £400-a-month mobile phone bills, the fact that she misses her old Tuesday night karaoke evenings with her mates and her understandable homesickness for Ireland, she reckons she's 'having the time of my life'.

But if she was granted one wish, this would be it:

'That everybody would treat each other equally,' she smiles. 'I hate it when people look down on other people because they don't do the same job or haven't got much money. Everyone is the same and everyone is successful in their own right if they're happy.'

Which must mean Keavy's the most successful person alive.

B*WITCHING FACTS ABOUT KEAVY . . .

* Keavy has problems sleeping at night unless the light is on. The poor love is scared of the dark!

* She has a tattoo on her left shoulder which symbolises happiness. She hid it from her parents for ages and ages because she thought they'd tell her off. As it happens, her mum and dad quite liked it.

* She blames herself for B*Witched's obsession with denim – she owns at least fifteen pairs and reckons she's a jeans-oholic.

* Keavy has a bit of a wonky finger – and Edele is responsible. Years ago, Edele slammed a car door on it and it's never been the same since. 'I think it broke,' Keavy groans, 'but I never had it fixed so now it's bent.'

* She once had her tongue pierced, but took it out because she couldn't eat her favourite grub. 'It didn't really hurt,' she says, 'but I had to eat soup for ages so I took it out.'

* The first record she bought was 'The Right Stuff' by New Kids On The Block.

* She likes 'Clean hair. Very clean hair.'

* Her favourite colour is purple!

* She is most likely to say, 'I haven't a notion' (one of her favourite phrases).

* Her motto is, 'You only live once – so go for it.'

CHAPTER FIVE

Sinead Maria O'Carroll

Nickname: Socky and Grenade
Birth date: 14 May 1978
Born: Dublin, Ireland
Star sign: Taurus

Like Lindsay, Sinead O'Carroll wasn't brought up in Dublin. She was born there alright, but when she was just a few months old she and her dad Eamonn (an electrician) and mum Barbara (who owns a lingerie shop) moved to Newbridge in County Kildare, a wee distance from Ireland's capital city.

She was the eldest child in the family (she has two sisters, Elaine and Ailish, and a brother, Paul) and reckons that it was because she was born first that she got a tough deal growing up.

'I was brought up quite well,' she says. 'I've got one brother and two sisters and I'm the eldest so that's why my parents were strict with me. I've always known what I wanted to do and I was always ambitious when I was younger. I think that kept me quite sensible and on the straight and narrow . . .

'My dad was very strict, though . . . I wasn't allowed out to discos or anything like that,' she smiles. 'But I don't really regret it. I suppose staying in meant that I could earn loads of money babysitting so I could afford to go to my dance classes. I also got to study, so I did very well in my exams. It paid off in the end.'

When she was growing up, Sinead was quite tiny, and because of this she thought that she was too small to get involved in a lot of activities at school (looking back, she realises how silly she was!). Despite that, she still managed to win a medal for hurdling and even managed to win an award for being Schoolgirl of the Year! What's more, in her transition year at school, she did something that she is still extremely proud of . . .

'I worked with handicapped children,' she explains. 'I'm proud I made them happy.'

Her musical interest began quite early on. She started dancing when she was four years old, and from the age of eight she took Irish dancing lessons with her sister Elaine.

'I went to lessons for seven years,' she smiles, 'and if anyone had told me I'd be Irish dancing to a pop song when I was older I would have thought they were absolutely mad!'

Her performing skills didn't stop there. In the summer holidays, when she wasn't at school, Sinead would take part in dance and drama workshops at Newbridge College and was over the moon when, at fifteen, she was chosen to play the wizard in the college production of *The Wizard of Oz*. It was at about this time that Sinead's parents decided to let her travel into the centre of Dublin on her own to take jazz dance and ballet lessons ('I felt so grown up,' she laughs).

'Like the other girls, I was tinkering about on the piano from seven or eight years old,' she smiles. 'Deep down inside I always had this feeling that this was going to happen to me. From the age of seven I imagined I'd be doing interviews one day. My mum used to say things like "Sinead, you're not on the stage now," but I'd be daydreaming and wouldn't really hear her.'

Despite being academic, Sinead wasn't always an angel, and once managed to get a serious ticking off at school for, er, throwing eggs over everyone in her class.

'It was the naughtiest thing I've ever done,' she grins, remembering the incident. 'And I got suspended for it.' Ouch. Luckily, the setback didn't stop her from getting on with her musical career.

When she was sixteen she was such a brilliant performer that she managed to win a scholarship, no less, to a dance and drama college called the London Studio, in the English capital.

'I did a year in college doing dancing, singing and drama, living in north London,' she smiles. 'Then when I came back to Ireland I was working in theatres all over Dublin!'

But her first brush with fame was actually quite accidental. She got interviewed in the street by a TV crew!

'I was caught by an Australian show like *Beadle's About*,' she explained to a journalist recently. 'A TV crew asked to interview me, but it was all in French, and an old lady gave me a very hard time!' Very strange . . .

Back in the real world(!) Sinead managed to get jobs at Dublin's Gate and Olympia theatres, and also managed to land herself a few parts as an extra on TV, as well as making a decent living working as a shop assistant and selling things over the telephone! Luckily, it wasn't too long before she met Edele, Keavy and Lindsay, and B*Witched was born.

'After we met in the studio we spent about four or five months training together every single day for about three hours,' she remembers. 'People used to say to us, "What are you doing in there?" and we were, like, "Well, we're just training for our dreams." We spent a lot of money in the beginning, but it's all paid off now.'

Despite the fact that B*Witched have had heaps of number ones, performed all over the world and have more fans than she could ever dream of, Sinead has still managed to keep her feet on the floor. 'I'm a Taurean, so I'm earthy and stubborn,' she says, explaining why she has managed to stay so down-to-earth. 'I'm practical and I'm also quite ambitious.'

No wonder, then, that she knows that being famous, on its own, won't make her happy.

'At the end of the day you have to make yourself happy, otherwise you'll be too dependent on other people,' she grins. 'You have to balance what you want, and right now my career is great.

'At the end of the day,' she smiles, 'I'm just an ordinary Irish girl.'

B*Witching facts about Sinead . . .

✳ Sinead is an excellent masseuse and is always giving the girls a backrub on the tour bus after shows.

* She still hasn't managed to pass her driving test, despite trying really hard. She took lessons for a while but gave up . . . because she was too frightened.

* She's the cook of the band and her favourite recipe is tagliatelle carbonara . . . which is tricky, as the other girls hate it!

* Her worst ever crime was nicking an envelope – but it was a genuine accident. 'I was busy buying stamps one day and I just forgot to pay for an envelope I grabbed,' she shrugs. Oops.

* She hates olives!

* Her worst habit is accidentally standing in front of the TV when the other girls are trying to watch it.

* She once gave an interview and realised at the end of it that one of her false nails had broken off and got stuck in her hair.

* She reckons that if all she had left in the world was a fiver, she'd spend it on a phone card to call her mum and dad.

* Her favourite colour is black!

* The first record she bought was 'Fame' by Irene Cara.

* She collects fake tattoo transfers.

* Not many people know this, but Sinead has a small scar on her hairline.

* She is most likely to say, 'You are not!' (It's her favourite phrase!)

* Her motto is, 'What comes around, goes around.'

CHAPTER SIX

The Lynch Mob

Of course, anyone who knows anything about pop music knows that Keavy and Edele were not the first people in their family to make it in the pop world. Their big brother Shane has been a member of Boyzone for years and has travelled the world promoting his band's hit records – and that's a lot of travelling, 'cause Boyzone have had number ones in zillions of countries.

Yet, despite his success, Shane had nothing whatever to do with the girls forming B*Witched or having lots of number one records (as you'll know if you've read the last five chapters of this book!). In fact, the girls were planning to be entertainers before Shane even dreamt of being in a band, and when he joined Boyzone the girls couldn't have been more shocked!

'We wanted to be in a pop band long before Shane showed any interest in it. We were quite surprised when he joined Boyzone because Shane was shy,' Keavy told Linda Duff of the *Star* when the girls first started out as Sassy.

'We always knew he was musical, but Boyzone was a big surprise. He was a real charmer as a boy. He was in the school choir so he sang from an early age and he was fit 'cause he was into BMX bikes and skateboarding. He could charm anybody with his smile.

'But he never opened any doors for us at home – and he certainly didn't open any in the music business!'

Obviously Keavy and Edele's lives did change quite dramatically when Boyzone became famous. For a start, BZ fans started hanging out around their house in Donaghmede. And whenever friends or people they met discovered that Shane was their brother, Keavy and Edele had to put up with all sorts of odd behaviour. ('They'd start screaming, which was a bit weird,' Edele laughs.) Apart from that, the biggest change was the fact that they hardly got to see their brother – he was too busy jet-setting the planet doing television shows, concerts and interviews.

But since B*Witched have become famous too, Shane has always been careful not to meddle in his little twin sisters' pop careers. He believes that the girls are managing just fine by themselves!

'He never interferes or tells us what to do, but we have learnt a lot from him by following his example,' Edele explains. 'He's taught us how to cope with missing the family, being away from home and how to work until you drop. We have seen what he's achieved and we've learnt a lot from it. He's a great role model for us.'

Weirdly, nearly every one of the Lynch children has made a career out of the music industry.

There's . . .

SHANE, 22, obviously in Boyzone.

KEAVY AND EDELE, our B*Witched heroines!

TARA, 24, who is in a band called Fab and is probably going to be a big pop star herself some day.

And . . .

NAOMI, 15, a dancer who came second in the European Dance Championship in Bristol last year.

In fact, the only member of the family who isn't dancing or singing for a living is . . .

ALISON, 23, who lives in America and works for a computer company. ('She's the brains of the family,' says Edele.)

Obviously, Mum and Dad Lynch, who are called Brendan and Noleen, are extremely happy about their children's success.

'I'm proud of them all,' Mrs Lynch says. 'We sent them all to singing and dancing lessons but what they've achieved is all their own doing.

'We always knew that the twins would go into show business but we never dreamed that they would end up on *Top of the Pops*. They sang in school and in the church choir but dancing was always their first love. No way would they ever sing in public as kids.'

Of course, there has been a wee downside to B*Witched and Boyzone's success – both Shane and Keavy worked as mechanics at Mr Lynch's garage, and left when they got their pop star jobs. Dad doesn't seem too put out about it though!

'My children are the hardest workers I ever came across,' he says. 'But when the music opportunities came up for both of them I told them to go for it. You don't get second chances in this life.'

There are some advantages to having your children in pop bands, of course, and for Edele and Keavy's mum one of the biggest is being able to watch her kids on telly to see if they're looking after themselves.

'I can tell whether they're eating well or whether they look upset or tired,' she reveals. 'Then I can phone them up and say, "Keavy, you look tired. Get you to bed and have an early night." I particularly like it when they perform live because I know they're really there.'

Number One Family!

The biggest moment of excitement in the Lynch family history has to be in June last year when both Boyzone and B*Witched managed to make it to the top of the British charts! B*Witched had their debut single, 'C'est La Vie', go straight into the charts at number one, while Boyzone's third album, *Where We Belong*, made it to the top of the album charts.

Keavy and Edele were obviously over the moon when the charts came out that Sunday, but were doubly delighted that their brother was celebrating too.

'We are so excited and Shane is even more excited for us than he was about his own number one,' Keavy told one reporter from the *Evening Standard*.

Mrs Lynch, meanwhile, was completely relieved, as she'd spent days on tenterhooks waiting to find out how her children's records would fare . . .

'Waiting for the charts to come out was awful,' said

Noleen. 'I couldn't sleep or eat for days!'

When the news was eventually revealed, there was so much commotion in the Lynch household that Keavy and Edele could hardly hear themselves speak on the phone.

'When I called home to break the news there was so much shouting and screaming at the other end that I had to ring off because I couldn't hear a thing,' Edele grins. 'I gave them half an hour to calm down, but when I called them back it was just the same!'

The day after the chart was unveiled, the Lynch twins flew into London to film *Top of the Pops*, and found themselves arriving at Heathrow airport to an impromptu celebration with their brother!

Shane told the story to London's *Evening Standard* newspaper:

'I had not seen the girls for weeks until I flew back from Italy just as they were coming in from Ireland on one of the next flights,' he laughed. 'I had no idea what country they were in until I ran into a friend on my way out of the airport and he said he was meeting my sisters, so I waited around for them. We had a bit of a hug and congratulated each other.'

'I always knew they could do it. I'm delighted for them even though they've started off a bit better than us – our first single only went in at number two!'

CHAPTER SEVEN

Love Spells . . .

You'd think the B*Witched girls, gorgeous as they are, would be inundated with flowers, cards and romantic offers from hunky boys from all corners of the globe, wouldn't you? You'd reckon that being in such a brilliant pop group and being such sparky, fun babes, there would be men queuing up for miles to whisk them off to posh restaurants and romantic holiday getaways. No such luck!

In fact, when one journalist mentioned this to Edele a few months ago, she nearly choked at how wrong the assumption was.

'Where's the queue actually?' she laughed. 'There's no one here today!'

The truth is that all four of the B*Witched girls are single, too busy with their jet-set, hard-working lives to even contemplate having boyfriends.

'Like a lot of modern women, we worked on Valentine's Day,' Sinead explained recently. 'It's difficult to find time to build a relationship. Anyway, when I do meet someone I like I'm always worried I'll be let down, so there's no one special yet.'

The problem is that the girls' hectic schedules don't allow them time even to meet boys, never mind date them. How can you have a boyfriend if he's stuck in Ireland and you're in America for eight weeks and then France, Germany and Italy after that? It's impossible!

'It's very hard in this business to meet someone special,' Sinead says. 'We normally only get the chance to say hello to someone for ten minutes at a gig and then don't get the opportunity to see them again for another two months. I'm so busy that I would never be able to fit anything in. However, hopefully things won't be like that forever.'

You won't see our B*Witchers crying about being single, though. All four of the girls seem quite happy with their single status – there's not one 'desperate' babe among them! As Keavy explains . . .

'Sometimes I'd like to have a boyfriend,' she admits, 'but I'm not looking for one because everyone knows if you look for a boyfriend you'll never find one. If I happen to meet the right person, then great, but I'm quite happy on my own, thank you!'

Edele agrees. 'None of us feels the need for a boyfriend. We're still young.'

'Yeah,' says Lindsay. 'We're having fun doing what we're doing. It's not like we need to go out with someone to be happy.'

That's not to say that they intend to remain single forever! One day, all of our B*Witchers would like to get married and have children . . . We can see it now: Edele with a pushchair, Keavy changing nappies, Sinead doing the school run and

Lindsay buying pretty dresses for her babies. (Although maybe not quite yet!)

'I'd like to settle down and get married one day,' says Sinead. 'But I'll have to fall in love first and someone'll have to fall in love with me, so it might be a long time! But I think if you really want to get married you have to work at making it happen.'

Edele agrees. 'It would be nice if we all found some real nice boys,' she smiles. 'If we find ourselves boyfriends it's gonna be because we've just met them and we've clicked straight away, not just because of who we are. We won't say no if it happens.'

'Anyway,' Sinead told a journalist, 'I'm waiting till I'm thirty. God knows who it'll be though. The next person who drops out of the sky. I'd love to have children but then I think of the pain. I can't even go to the dentist.'

Most of the girls were in relationships before they were in B*Witched so they know all about the trials and tribulations involved in being in love with someone.

Edele, for instance, had a boyfriend in Dublin before she moved to England, but realised after a while that it was the right thing to do to split up with him.

'In any relationship you need to have time together,' she says. 'And since the group moved to England I couldn't be with him any more. It didn't make sense to carry on with him in Dublin and me here.'

Lindsay, meanwhile, was quite happy to get rid of her ex. In an interview with *Now!* magazine she reckoned that her boyfriend had been quite bad to her and that she relished the opportunity to get rid of him!

'I don't want to go into personal details here,' she said, 'but he was mean, a real meaner. He was so naughty to me. That's how you can tell I'm not a real witch. If I was, I'd have turned him into a frog right then!'

Sinead was a bit luckier with her last long-term boyfriend. She described the relationship to a journalist from *Smash Hits* as a 'fairy-tale' romance.

'I went out with a guy for two and a half years and we never had one fight,' she smiled, remembering. 'He'd do anything for me. Looking back on it now, the only thing about it was that it was a bit monotonous, very routine. I was about sixteen when we started going out and, no, I'm not telling you his name!'

If the girls did decide it was time to find love, Edele reckons she'd be in serious trouble. And why?

'Because I can't flirt!' she explains. 'I've only had someone ask me to dinner once and that was years ago when I was working in the sports shop!'

Lindsay, on the other hand, reckons she's got this flirting malarkey down to a T.

'I can be a bit of a flirt,' she says. 'I make loads of eye contact, smile and mess about in a jokey way. But I don't believe in chat up lines though,' she adds. 'I crack jokes instead!'

Sinead, however, goes for the simple approach. 'If I meet a boy I like I just try to make eye contact,' she laughs. 'And I'll go out of my way to try and have a chat with them!'

So that's where we've been going wrong . . .

Boys that bewitch B*Witched!

If the girls weren't so busy, and actually wanted to have relationships, they have very definite ideas about the kind of guys they'd go for.

Edele, for instance, quite likes Jason Priestley, but she fancies another famous bloke, too. 'I've got the hots for David Charvet who used to be in *Baywatch*,' she admits. 'He's very cute and sporty as well.'

But she doesn't really seem too fussy.

'Men look better when they're scruffy or dirty,' she says. 'As long as their socks are clean I'm not bothered!' And there's one more quality a potential boyfriend for Edele would have to have – he must be punctual!

Lindsay, on the other hand, is less sure of the kind of guy she'd go for.

'I really don't know who my ideal man would be,' she smiles. 'He'd have to have a great personality and everything and I don't know anyone famous well enough to be able to tell. If I was going on looks alone I'd have to be really boring and say Brad Pitt. I know everyone likes him but he's lovely.'

And if Brad decided that he wanted to woo our Lindsay (Jennifer Anniston aside) he'd have to be quite romantic 'cause our Lindsay is a sucker for hearts and flowers.

'I like little things like sending cards for no reason,' she says. 'It's so romantic.'

What she looks for in a man is someone who is caring, thoughtful and has ambition.

Keavy meanwhile prefers men who aren't too macho.

'I like a man who shows his emotions,' she said recently.

'Someone who wouldn't be scared to cry in front of me. I also like a man who makes me laugh.

'I think everyone wants to get married. Don't they? I'd love to be in love with someone – I wouldn't care whether he was the paperboy or what he did.'

Keavy reckons the most romantic thing any boy ever did for her was to buy her flowers and a cute teddy bear. But if someone was to try to woo her that way again he'd have to make sure he made her laugh and would let her look after him!

Sinead, finally, reckons she'll eventually fall for someone who is spontaneous and who would give her lots of affection. 'Just a nice, loving man,' she smiles.

Boys? We think it's time you formed that orderly queue!

The girls' first kisses

Keavy's first ever kiss was with a guy called Dax who happened to be a Portuguese friend of her elder brother Shane. 'I remember being very nervous,' she says. 'I was about twelve.'

Lindsay's first kiss was on a school bus when she was at school, with a boy called Nico. 'We dated until the summer,' she laughs. 'Then we hated each other.' Hmm, true love!

Edele's first shot at snogging came when she was still a schoolkid, with (another!) mate of Shane's called Christopher. 'I met him BMX-ing,' she says. She quickly followed that one up by kissing a boy called Patrick who happened to be the only boy in her metalwork class who would talk to her (because she was a girl). What a nice chap!

Last but not least, Sinead remembers her first kiss extremely well. She shared it with a lad called James who was playing violin in a show that she was in. 'I went out with him for about eight months!' she remembers.

CHAPTER EIGHT

Eternal Fame

I thought fame might change me as a person, but it hasn't – not even slightly. It made us excited for a while and we were proud that we'd achieved what we set out to do, but it didn't really change us as people. Edele

It happens to the best of people when they become famous: it doesn't matter how nice, gentle, or amiable they are when they start out on the road to pop-superstardom, fame seems to change them. A sweet young girl can turn into a power-hungry vixen. A pleasant, charming boy can turn into the kind of greedy young pup you'd like to slap sideways with a meat cleaver. For some terrible reason, when people become famous, the pressure of fans, constant media intrusion and exhausting schedules tends to have horrible effects on pop stars – instead of wising up, they seem to harden up.

There are hundreds of disappointed fans out there who can relate sad stories to you: how they met their idols backstage and found them to be condescending or uninterested; how they asked for an autograph only to get an angry stare and the brush-off. At the end of the day, the old warning of 'never meet your idols' generally makes sense: they often turn out to be not the people you hoped they were.

It's not surprising then that some of the journalists, radio DJs and record company execs who work with B*Witched were expecting their amazing rise to fame to alter the girls for the worse – but it just hasn't happened.

'They're the same as they ever were,' says a pop journalist who meets the girls for interviews from time to time. 'If anything, they've become happier than they were in the beginning. I think that seeing their dreams come true has made them brighter, sparkier people.

'I remember I interviewed them once last year when Lindsay was suffering from a terrible bout of 'flu, probably due to all the hard work they'd recently put in, but despite the fact that she looked like she wanted to vomit she still managed to give me a cheery smile and was very enthusiastic when it came to answering my questions.'

Famous, us?

The fact is that fame is something that the B*Witched girls enjoy, and their management team and record company work so well with them that they never become too exhausted to enjoy their success.

Fame is something that doesn't faze the girls in the slightest. They never really go to pop star parties, definitely don't subscribe to the rock and roll lifestyle (they're too busy staying fit and keeping their heads together) and generally treat their work as 'the best job in the world' (but a job all the same!). They find it very difficult to get their heads around the fact that they're pop stars and that half the world wants to meet them.

'I think I first realised I was a pop star when I heard we were number one,' says Lindsay. 'I suppose that makes you a pop star. But I still can't think of myself as a pop star though. It's weird. You don't change but the things around you do.'

By the things around you she probably means the limos, the hotels, the travelling and the way that people suddenly start to treat you with a little more awe than they did in the past. But, to be honest, the four B*Witchers hardly notice these trivial things at all.

'I'm not sure anyone ever feels famous at all,' Sinead told a journalist recently. 'You don't feel any different inside – you're just the same person. You don't wake up one morning and think, "Aha. Now I'm famous."'

So how have the girls manage to succeed where so many others have failed? How have they managed to remain lovely people – despite their record-breaking success – when so many other pop bands before them have fallen out, had tantrums and generally become the kind of people you wouldn't want to sit next to on a crowded bus?

Keavy thinks their upbringing might have something to do with it.

'I suppose the fact that we share the same values has something to do with our Catholic upbringing,' she says. 'It gives you a sense of who you are and a respect for yourself and for other people.'

It obviously works. B*Witched are possibly the most fan-friendly band in the charts. Instead of seeing autograph hunters as a hassle, they positively revel in meeting people and making new friends.

'We just love meeting the fans,' said Edele in a recent interview, 'Whether they're five or fifty, as long as we're giving pleasure to people, then we're happy. We have a lot of parents coming up to us and saying how glad they are that we are role models for their kids.'

Keavy also adores meeting her fans.

The girls manage to lead relatively normal lives and up until recently they managed to travel without the aid of a pack of burly security guards. If people write letters to Edele or Keavy at their Irish home, Mrs Lynch sometimes manages to find the time to send them autographs, and Sinead reckons that she can still pop into London on the tube without even being recognised. Abroad it can sometimes be a little harder though. The band have recounted how in Singapore they encountered a pack of fans who knocked on the door of every room in their hotel until they found the B*Witchers. And in Rome the girls met a group of fans who followed them everywhere, sometimes arriving at the band's next destination before they did!

But B*Witched really don't mind. As far as they're concerned, at the end of the day the people they're meeting are just saying 'thank you for your music' and that's the greatest honour anyone could give them. (Well, sometimes they do find weird ways of saying it – someone once sent Sinead a pack of butter as a gift. Bizarre!)

Fame for B*Witched, then, is a nice thing that affects everyone around them, not the girls themselves.

'Although there is an upside to being famous,' says Sinead. 'We get free clothes and people pay for our dinner.' Not bad, eh?

Since they've hit the big time the girls have only done one naughty thing: they nicked Boy George's mascara! The four B*Witchers were playing on the same bill as him at London's Grand Theatre when the incident in question took place.

'Boy George was really nice and lent us his mascara,' Lindsay explained to a tabloid.

'We promised to give it back but we never did!' The rotters.

Still, compared to some of the japes that other bands get up to, the great mascara theft will hardly even get a mention in the annals of rock 'n' roll debauchery, we think!

The Backlash

What the girls haven't managed to escape is the usual rubbish that happens to any band when they get famous: the backlash. The backlash usually occurs when a band get so big that they don't get time to do interviews any more, and the press, so desperate to get stories on them, either weed out some silly little thing and blow it up out of all proportion – or just make up lies!

Luckily, the B*Witched girls have absolutely nothing to hide, so their backlash has been so tiny that it hardly even warrants a mention.

The first thing that really hit the headlines was after an

article appeared in *Now!* magazine in which the girls confided to a journalist that they'd used a white witch to help them cast spells to bring them good luck with their career.

'She's more of a fairy godmother really,' Edele had told the mag's journalist. 'She's called Titania and she's taught us a few spells for joy, good luck, health, happiness and wealth.'

She went on to explain how Titania had given them candles and ribbons in seven colours of the rainbow for a spell that took seven days to cast.

When the journalist asked them if the spell had helped 'C'est La Vie' make it to the top, the girls laughed hysterically.

'Well, the success of the record might have something to do with the four months' promotion work we did in night-clubs and schools, on the radio and on a stadium tour with 911,' Sinead scoffed a tad sarcastically.

The story about the witch had been a bit of fun and none of the girls meant any harm by it, but within weeks one tabloid newspaper had managed to stir up a bit of trouble for the B*Witchers. It reported how 'the Catholic Church' had 'gone mad' about the girls saying they'd consulted a witch (Hang on a sec! Didn't the girls say she was more of a fairy godmother?!), and quoted a church spokesman from Dublin as saying, 'It was an irresponsible gimmick.'

Hmmm.

Big Breakfast presenter Johnny Vaughan was, surprisingly, one of the people who decided to give B*Witched a hard time when they made it big.

'He described us as OK wallpaper,' Edele laughed,

recounting his snide remarks later. 'He said you wouldn't notice us when you walked into a room. He isn't exactly our biggest fan. When we were recording the *Top of the Pops* Christmas special we even overheard him saying to someone that he loved the Spice Girls for knocking us off the number one spot. Isn't that mean?'

Just a tad.

If that wasn't enough, in June 1998 the papers all gleefully reported how B*Witched had been 'dropped' from a Hanson concert (they were due to support the boys) later that week, and replaced by an unknown band called Hillman Minx. Hanson's manager reportedly said that they thought a live band would fit their show better. The papers said it was a snub. B*Witched hardly spent nights awake worrying about it!

The final stab came when the *Daily Star* ran a piece insisting that Sinead was twenty-five, not twenty (as if anyone cares!) – a fact that she has hotly disputed.

Still, the newspapers have had a hard time trying to find (or make up!) bad stories about the girls and have had a much better time finding nice ones. For instance, last year the *Daily Telegraph* ran a lovely story explaining how one fan, Charlie Roberts, who queued in the rain for five hours to watch B*Witched, later found out that the girls had prepared for the concert in her bedroom!

Charlie, who'd gone to see the girls perform, went back to her home in Leeds just to have her mum tell her that the group had spent two hours in her bedroom, singing and using her lipstick and hair lacquer (imagine that!). The band members had sought refuge in a pub when rain had disrupted a television interview and Charlie's mum, Elaine, was in the pub and invited them to use her house.

'I couldn't believe it because I had just seen them on stage,' Charlie told the *Telegraph*'s reporter. But her mum had managed to get video shots of the girls in the bedroom saying 'Hello, Charlie!' and the record company arranged for her to meet the girls at a later date.

You get the picture! B*Witched are nice girls, and scurrilous journos have a terrible time finding nasty stuff to print about them.

'There are no skeletons in our closet,' Edele says. 'You can have a look if you want, but you won't find any!'

Generally, fame is not a big hassle at all for Edele, Sinead, Keavy and Lindsay. In fact, it's a positive experience.

'Being a pop star is a twenty-four-hour job,' Edele admits. 'But it's never annoyed me.'

Perhaps the final word in this section should go to Lindsay, who told this story to journalist Johnny Dee while she was trying to explain what fame meant to her:

'When we were doing a schools tour in England we went to this school and there was a boy – he was a slow learner and he couldn't write very well,' she explained. 'After we'd performed his teacher burst in with this letter and said, "I can't really believe it. He sat down at his desk and wrote this in five minutes flat." And the note said, "I love you, you're brilliant, you made me so happy." Just to know you have that effect on people because of what you do for a living is brilliant . . .'

CHAPTER NINE

Magical Music . . .

B*Witched always knew that the first few months after they signed their record contract would be head-wreckingly busy. What they didn't realise, however, was how much they'd manage to achieve in such a short space of time!

Almost immediately after they signed their contract, Keavy, Edele, Lindsay and Sinead embarked on their first proper tour – supporting 911 – and played at some of the largest venues in Britain. It was an amazing time. As per usual, the girls had very little time to prepare for the tour and managed to polish up their songs and dance routines in about two days!

Still, the tour was a great success, and once it had finished the girls were ready to show what they could do to the ladies and gentlemen of the press! To publicise the band, B*Witched's record company, Epic, hired out a venue in London called The Talk of London and invited every important pop person – from the journalists at *Smash Hits* and *TV Hits* to the people at MTV – to come along and see what the girls could actually do.

That night, supported by their families (who had flown

over from Dublin specially for the event) B*Witched performed one of the most important gigs of their lives, complete with huge pyrotechnic glitter explosions for their finale. The press were amazed by what they saw and knew there and then that B*Witched were a force to be reckoned with.

All the four girls needed to do now was release a record! On 25 May 1998, B*Witched's first single, 'C'est La Vie', was unleashed on an expectant record-buying public . . . and the whole of Britain went crazy for it.

'We wanted to sing about being young, fresh and happy,' Edele told a journalist at the time. ' "C'est La Vie" is exactly all those things rolled into one. It's about having a good time.'

'It's a song that could be interpreted a number of different ways,' she told another reporter. 'But we see it as a kind of modern fairy tale – a song about being young and innocent. Which is pretty much how we feel at this time in our lives.'

If that was the case, everyone in Britain must have been having the time of their lives – because the single managed to sell more than 800,000 copies. And that wasn't all.

That Sunday, when the charts were unveiled, it turned out that B*Witched's first ever single had gone straight in at number one! It was astounding.

'We'd imagined all sorts of things would happen – like getting a record deal and going into the studio,' Sinead recalled later. 'But we never imagined going straight in the charts at number one, like that. When it finally sank in there was a lot of screaming and crying to be heard.'

It seemed that B*Witched's particular brand of pop – termed by the girls 'Irish hip-hop-pop' – was exactly what we'd been waiting for! The evening after the girls found out they were number one, their record company took them out to dinner at Planet Hollywood in London for a celebratory slap-up meal.

Busy B*s

Of course, once B*Witched had scored their first number one British single, everyone from Lands End to John O'Groats wanted to know who the girls were and see them perform. Almost instantly, the Irish foursome found themselves with packed schedules and even more tightly packed suitcases, travelling all over the country to do interviews, showcases and TV appearances. The girls may have had a number one single, but they knew that this was not a time to be resting on their laurels. If they wanted to maintain their chart success, there was hard work to do, and that meant getting straight into the preparations for their next single, 'Rollercoaster'.

The song ('about being happy-go-lucky through the ups and downs of life,' as Sinead explained it) was to be released in September, but there was a lot of work to be done – and the first thing they had to do was make a video. The director for the video decided he wanted the girls to 'fly' in the clip, and that meant that the girls had to spend hours attached to special harnesses. It was tricky stuff, and quite tiring, but when the girls saw the video they knew it was worth it – it was incredible.

When the single was eventually released on 21 September that year, B*Witched's fans were as mad about it as they were for 'C'est La Vie', and, yet again, the song charted . . . at number one. The girls must have felt like they were living in a dream.

As if things couldn't get better, just two weeks later Epic released B*Witched's debut album, and to celebrate the success of their special pop fairies they held a swanky do at a trendy London restaurant called The Collection.

The girls rubbed shoulders with celebrities, such as 911 and Steps, and partied with their families – Edele and Keavy's big brother Shane made the trip to London especially for the do. And the girls obviously loved every minute of it.

'We're totally enjoying the ride at the moment,' they told *OK!* magazine, who attended the launch. 'We totally believe in what we do and in the power of pop music to raise people's spirits. If we can do that then we're achieving our ambition.'

As an extra 'well-done' to the girls, Epic presented them with Prada rucksacks . . . sorely needed rucksacks, it turned out, as having conquered England B*Witched were about to embark on a special publicity tour around the world and back – to Australia, New Zealand, Japan, Singapore and the USA!

'It's been a brilliant day,' they said before they left the party, 'and we'd like to thank our fans for their support. If we've got a message in our music it's basically to live your life to the full. That's essentially what we're about.'

Four girls . . . four number ones . . .

When the girls left their special party, they had no idea that they were set to make history in a way that no other pop band ever had – not even the Beatles. As they set off to conquer the world, they continued to release records: 'To You I Belong', released on 7 December, just in time for Christmas, was their first ballad and managed to get them a hat trick – their third number one single. The icing on the cake was that, on the day they found out they'd gone straight to the top of the charts (again!), they also managed to scoop a prize at the prestigious *Smash Hits* pop awards.

'It's kind of unbelievable and completely overwhelming,' Sinead said a few weeks later. 'People tell us that they see and hear us everywhere but we don't know because we're working all the time. We found out that we'd got our third number one at last month's *Smash Hits* awards. We were getting ready for the show when we got the call. It was a really good feeling. We had a double celebration because we won best new act and got a number one hit!'

But the best was yet to come. The thing that really put them in pop's history books was what happened when they released their fourth single, 'Blame it on the Weatherman', in March 1999. Like the other three records, the song went straight to the top – and broke all records. Not even the Spice Girls had managed such a feat (their first six singles all reached number one but didn't go straight to the top, like our B*Witchers'!). And the Beatles' first song, 'Love Me Do', didn't even make the top ten! If we hadn't known it before, we certainly knew it now: B*Witched were a band in a million.

The luck of the Irish

So what is it about B*Witched's music that makes it so special? Sinead reckons she has the answers . . .

'People's perceptions of the Irish scene are always beardy types,' she told the *Guardian* newspaper. 'Traditional Irish music hadn't been done by a young group before so it was a challenge to us.'

She told a journalist from *OK!* magazine that it was the Irish sound that set B*Witched apart.

'I think that Boyzone initially opened the door for commercial success for Irish bands,' she explained. 'There's a lot of talent there. Music is a very prominent force in Dublin and in the west of Ireland. Every child has some connection with music because they either learn a musical instrument or go to dancing class . . .'

. . . just like our four B*Witchers!

But being in B*Witched means something more to the girls than just being Irish. They reckon their music sums up an attitude that a lot of music lovers can identify with.

'All the stuff we write is based on our own experience. We are writing songs from the viewpoint of late-teenagers,' Edele explained to reporters. 'We're cheeky and we're giddy on life. But we're not Bad Girls. We just believe in enjoying life to the max and we want to get that feeling over in our songs.

'We are four girls who happen to be in a band together.

We don't want to be one-dimensional. We don't want to be about one thing. We want to be about everything. We want B*Witched to be nothing less than a celebration of being alive.'

No one could deny that 1998 had been B*Witched's year. Less than twelve months later, with four number ones tucked under their belt, and a legion of fans going mad for the girls, Keavy, Edele, Lindsay and Sinead could hardly believe that they were the same four girls who had spent nights working in the Digges Lane dance studio 'training for their dreams'. The training had obviously paid off!

CHAPTER TEN

B*Witchingly Gorgeous . . .

The B*Witched girls are definitely magical creatures. They may look like pretty pixies, and dance like leaping leprechauns – but they definitely dress like 'jean-ies' (Groan).

Yup, ever since the B*Witched girls released 'C'est La Vie', the girls have been decked out in all sorts of delicious denim. From jeans to jackets, skirts to waistcoats, everything is stamped with their denim trademark.

It wasn't always like that. In their first incarnation, as Sassy, the girls had publicity shots taken wearing girly shirts and ties!

'It's changed drastically since we formed the band,' Lindsay admits. 'Now we've got a stylist who does our shopping for us. Out went the glam skirts and shoes. In came jeans and trainers. I've got a brand new wardrobe full of them.'

The denim wardrobe came about when the girls had a meeting with their record company to talk about their image.

All four of them decided that denim was something they all loved wearing and felt comfortable in – so denim it was.

'I think because we wear denim that's why we often get called a tomboy band,' Edele says. 'It makes us different from all other pop groups and it actually does suit our personalities.'

Denim is also easy to buy. For instance, on a recent trip to America, the girls stumbled across a warehouse in New Jersey full of fantastic – and cheap – denim get-up!

'They had loads of denim in this warehouse,' Lindsay says, 'and it was dead cheap. We were in our element!'

Of course, no matter how natural the B*Witched look is, the girls are the first to admit that their clothes, make-up sessions and hair-styling make them look a lot more glamorous than they are in real life.

'When we flick through magazines sometimes we have to laugh at the pictures of us,' Keavy says. 'Now if I see myself in the mirror without make-up I hardly know the face.'

The professional image consultants obviously do their work well – the clothes are gorgeous, the girls' hair is always perfect and their make-up looks fantastic – but at the end of the day, what really makes Edele, Keavy, Sinead and Lindsay look as fantastic as they do . . . is their good health sense. For a start, they are well known for not drinking alcohol.

'I haven't had a drink since New Year's Eve,' said Keavy in December 98. 'None of us drink, really. We just don't like it.'

Other than that, the girls always make sure they go to bed

early and drink lots of calcium enriched milk!

The very idea of them going out partying until the early hours and getting squiffy on champagne is ridiculous, they reckon. They don't even like clubbing ('We only listened to the dance remix of 'C'est La Vie' once,' laughs Keavy, wrinkling her nose) and they prefer to keep their feet on the ground rather than pretend to be rock-star big shots!

'If one of us had come into the band with the idea of party, party, party, let's go out drinking, that person wouldn't be in the band,' says Sinead. 'None of us is looking for that rock 'n' roll, glitz 'n' glam thing. We're the new generation of pop star.'

'It's true,' says Edele. 'Even after the Royal Variety Performance we did, we went straight to bed.' She smiles. 'Looking after yourself, eating properly and taking vitamins makes you perky.'

And perkiness is what B*Witched have – in vat loads.

What the girls have said about lookin' spellbinding . . .

Edele: 'The best aid to looking good is confidence. It's the sexiest thing in the world and if you believe you look good yourself, boys instantly think you're more attractive.'

Sinead: 'The first thing I always do in the morning when I wake up is apply a thin layer of cucumber eye-gel. It tightens up the skin around the eyes and helps get rid of bags from all the late nights we have.'

Hands up who's going to be famous!

The Girls...

Keavy-Jane Elizabeth Annie Lynch

Edele
Claire
Christina
Edwina
Lynch

Sinead
Maria
O'Carroll

Lindsay
Gael
Christina
Elaine
Armaou

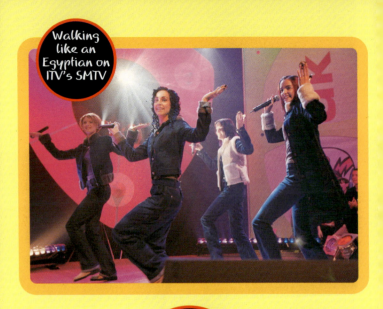

Walking like an Egyptian on ITV's SMTV

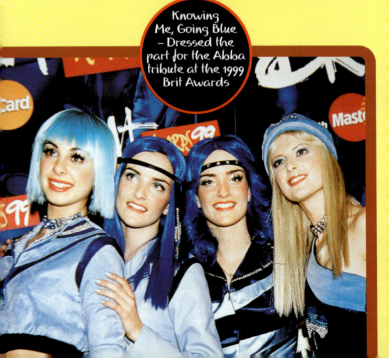

Knowing Me, Going Blue – Dressed the part for the Abba tribute at the 1999 Brit Awards

Best of pals

Denim-clad in the park

All glammed up at the BRMB Awards

Jumping for joy at the Capital Radio Extravaganza in London

Keavy: 'You'll always look good if you get enough sleep. I need at least eight hours a night or else I can't function the next day and I look terrible! At the end of a really busy day, I like to spray my feet with this foot spray I get. It's really relaxing and freshens you up. Oh, and wearing a nice perfume makes me feel nice too. I love Christian Dior's Dune.'

Lindsay: 'Basically I love my make-up – I can't help it. I've got absolutely tons of the stuff. I've got a whole bag of foundations and concealers, one for powders and another one for eye-shadows and pencils! But I always make sure I take off all my make-up and cleanse every night before I go to bed. Drinking plenty of water keeps your skin really clear and free from spots too.'

All about Lindsay's magical hair

Lindsay hasn't always had dark curly hair. She was born with a head of jet black hair, but it gradually got lighter and very, very curly, so by the time she was four she had blonde ringlets! As she got older it changed again, and when she was twelve her hair had become long, dark and very straight. Then, when she moved to Ireland, it went curly again (must be the Irish mist!). Her natural hair colour nowadays is medium brown, but she dyes it black. Maybe when she washes it out she'll find that her hair's gone red – or even green!

'If I'm not working I don't care what my hair looks like,'

she laughs. 'I just stick a hat or gel on it. When we're working, though, it takes us four hours to have our hair and make-up done, 'cause there's only one make-up artist between us!'

Get fit the Pixie way!

Believe it or not, the B*Witched girls don't really work out – they hardly have time! But as Edele says, 'We do so much dancing we don't need to.'

'There's never a long period when we're not jumping around or doing something active,' says Keavy. 'I'm okay though because I can eat as much as I like and never put weight on.' Alright for some, eh?

Lindsay used to play a lot of netball when she was younger and, of course, she kick-boxed with the twins back in Ireland, but nowadays she just doesn't have the time for organised sport.

'I always try to have a swim if we're staying in a hotel with a pool though,' she smiles. 'Otherwise, generally we manage to keep fit doing our everyday things like performing.'

Here are the girls' top three tips for keeping mind, body and soul together:

1) GET LOTS OF SLEEP

'I just don't understand people who can stay up late,' Edele says. 'We get as much sleep as we possibly can, just to recharge our batteries.'

2) DON'T SMOKE

'Ugh! Smoking's disgusting,' says Keavy. Enough said.

3) EAT ALL THE RIGHT THINGS

'Make sure you eat well,' says Edele, 'because when you do, your skin and hair look so much better – although since we're always on the go it can be difficult to do that.'

There you go, then! Follow the B*Witched top three health tips and you too will be dancing leprechaun-like into the next millennium!

Six steps to enchanting style!

1) YOU DON'T NEED TO BE SKIMPY TO LOOK SEXY!

B*Witched prove that you don't have to wear skimpy dresses and tottery heels to look gorgeous! Like our four girls, you can wear jeans, skinny-rib T-shirts and trainers and still look a million dollars (without worrying about slipping over on silly high heels!). The way the B*Witched girls make their denim look glam is by carefully applying fresh make-up and glamming up their clothes with cheap-but-glitzy accessories, like pretty earrings and hair clips.

2) JAZZ UP YOUR JEANS!

Jeans are possibly the cheapest and longest-lasting items of clothing you could possibly wear – so they're the most economical way to dress. B*Witched always have denim on their legs – so how come their jeans always look that little bit spicier than your average pair of trews? Well, the girls' stylist manages to shop around for different pairs, but you can get the same look by doing a bit of DIY. Save your old jeans and update them by sewing on sequins, beads, ribbons and patches. You could even paint patterns on the bottoms of the legs by using fabric paints.

3) BRUSH UP YOUR BARNET!

All of the B*Witched girls have simple hairdos, but manage to change them with plaits, slides and coloured streaks. Luckily, you can buy most of the things they use very cheaply in chemists and accessory shops. Hair mascara is a must if you want to go for the girls' blue and purple hair streaks. Meanwhile, braiding your hair costs nothing! Plait a few strands of hair at the front of your face, and fasten them with jazzy pieces of gold thread or tiny hair clips!

4) GO GLITTERATI!

The B*Witched girls seem to sprinkle fairy dust wherever they go! Glitter is a huge part of their look (they even sprinkle glitter stars on their dressing room floors for good luck!), so go glitzy and add some sparkle into your make-up routine. There are lots of sparkly eye-shadows and tubes of body and face glitter available in the shops for just a couple of pounds, so save up and shine on, sista!

5) GO EASY ON THE MAKE-UP!

None of the B*Witched girls slap on their make-up – they

use it for a more natural glowing look, so they look perfect, not painted.

'When you're putting your make-up on always be very sparing,' says Sinead, 'because it can make you look really cheap if you don't go easy. Oh, and if you haven't got much money to spend on make-up, here's a good tip when your mascara's running out: put a drop of water in it.'

6) BODY ART

If you like Sinead's tattoo, you can fake it easily by buying one of the brilliant temporary tattoo kits available on the market, or by having a henna tattoo done, which lasts just a matter of weeks. The best part about these alternatives is that they're not permanent – which means you can chop and change your mind and try different patterns whenever you so desire!

CHAPTER ELEVEN

Astral Travelling!

Pack up your suitcases and jump on your broomsticks – because if you want to be like B*Witched, you've got to see the world!

Ever since the girls first made it big, they've been jumping on trains, planes and automobiles to travel to all four corners of the globe in a bid to sell their records.

Over the last year and a bit, the girls have literally B*Witched the planet. Their passports are brimming with stamps from every country in Europe and beyond, they've met people speaking over twelve different languages and have been on more flights than a NASA astronaut!

The truth is that the girls are now so well travelled they could easily present their own holiday show. Just mention a country to them and they'll be able to tell you what it's like, whether the food was any good, and exactly what they did there.

Travelling is probably the biggest change that being famous has made to the girls' lives. They thought they were being adventurous enough when they first moved to England, just a few years ago, to begin their pop careers.

Little did they know then that by the end of their first year they'd have become seasoned world-wide travellers.

It's a good job that they love it!

'Travelling is almost like flicking through a real-life holiday brochure,' says Lindsay. 'You get to see all these really great places, but really quickly!'

'It's great,' says Keavy. 'I think getting to meet so many interesting people is really cool. Everyone's been really nice to us and given us a lot of support wherever we've been. We've made some really lovely friends.'

Edele thinks they're the most fortunate girls in the world.

'I do,' she says. 'I feel like we're really lucky to be seeing all these amazing places while we're so young.'

'Yeah,' says Sinead. 'And we've seen places we once only dreamed of seeing. Touring the States has been a dream come true for me. I've always wanted to go.'

It may be great fun, but travelling the B*Witched way is a million miles from the holidays that you may have been lucky enough to go on with your families. For a start, whenever the girls go anywhere they have to work – they have relatively little time for sightseeing or sunbathing! Secondly, with most of the countries they visit, B*Witched can stay for only a few days, while they do their TV appearances and interviews, before jetting off to some other far-flung destination to work (they are too busy to hang around). This means that the girls often only get a chance to see the airport, their hotel rooms, and the TV studio where they have to work, before packing up their suitcases and the Prada rucksacks they were given by their record company, and heading off to the airport again.

But perhaps the most important difference between B*Witched's travels and your summer holiday travels is that when you travel you have time to prepare; B*Witched, on the other hand, seem to travel at the weirdest times, fitting flights in between rehearsals, interviews and recording!

For instance, the day before the girls flew to Australia in 1998 they had to record the video for 'To You I Belong'. This meant that they were up at 5.00am one day, shooting the video for twenty-four hours until 5.00am the next day (there was no time to sleep!), and then they managed to grab three hours of rest at their hotel before catching a twenty-two-hour flight (Get that? Twenty-two hours!) to Oz. You'll understand, then, why they slept all the way!

'The schedules are always very busy,' Sinead told a journalist recently. 'We've been all around Europe and to New York, New Zealand and Australia. We're off to Japan next week then we're going back to Italy for the MTV awards.'

Phew! Like we said, it certainly isn't a package holiday.

Perhaps the hardest thing for the girls to deal with when they travel is the fact that they're so far from their emerald isle: they miss Ireland like crazy. All four of the girls admit that when they get tired, grumpy, bored or restless, the first things they pine for are their friends and family back home.

'You forget how much you love your home town – until you move away,' Keavy told a pop journalist once, during a rare moment in which she was relaxing at home in Ireland. 'I can relax here, see my family, hang out with my friends. You know, just be normal.'

Lindsay emphasised the point:

'I know it sounds really sad but I don't think I've found anywhere in the world that beats where I live in Ireland,' she smiled lovingly. 'It's always really great to come back home.'

Still, the girls know that Ireland's always there for them to return home to. And if they ever hang up their pop star hats and return to Dublin to retire (not yet, we hope!) Lindsay, Keavy, Sinead and Edele will have plenty of memories of their travels to relate to their hubbies, children and grandkids!

Here are some that we're sure they'll look back at fondly . . .

Places the girls have B*Witched!

AUSTRALIA

Edele and Keavy had always wanted to go to Australia, so when they went there in '98 they were over the moon with excitement. They visited the country's most famous city – Sydney – and then headed to Victoria to visit the province's biggest metropolis, Melbourne.

'You know what, there's always little differences between countries, but everywhere is basically the same,' Lindsay told *Smash Hits* once the girls had arrived there. 'Like, if I look out the window here in Melbourne I can see big buildings, a big bridge and a river. It could be anywhere – Sydney, New York, even London.'

Keavy reckons she fell in love with the place.

'I thought the people were great,' she told *TV Hits* magazine later. 'They were very friendly and hospitable.'

NEW ZEALAND

It took just a quick flight from Australia to get the girls to the lush green mountains and valleys of New Zealand. The girls managed to spend a bit of time in Auckland, the country's capital city, and found that the thing they loved about the country – even more than the fresh air and countryside – was the people.

'New Zealanders are just like Irish people,' said Edele later. 'They have the same sense of humour!'

No wonder they loved it!

THE USA

The four B*Witchers managed to see a lot of the USA when they supported the band 'N Sync on their American tour. The girls' favourite place, however, seemed to be the Big Apple, a.k.a. New York!

'Everything is just so big in New York,' Lindsay laughed at the time. 'The buildings are huge, the streets are bigger and the portions of food are ginormous! Everything's just so big, and that includes the people's personalities. They're all like, "Hey! How ya doing!" But they're quite sweet!'

Perhaps another reason the girls will never forget New York was that they managed to spend St Patrick's Day there in 1999 – and a fantastic time was had by all.

ENGLAND

England may not seem a million miles away from Dublin (in fact, London is just an hour's flight from Ireland's capital city) but when the girls had to move to the UK after signing their record deal, it seemed like they were emigrating to the other side of the world! Edele, Keavy, Sinead and Lindsay are Irish girls through and through, and living in London was probably like landing on another planet.

Keavy, for one, had a terrible time getting to grips with the city's underground system. On one shopping trip she managed to lose the other girls, and it took her about three hours to find the way back to their house on her own. But it wasn't such a terrible experience. Y'see, by the time she got back home, the other three had cooked her dinner!

JAPAN

When B*Witched first hit the Far East they weren't sure what to expect. But the moment they flew into Japan they knew it was a special place and they fell in love with the polite Japanese people, the incredible electronic gadgets and the country's customs.

One thing they weren't so in love with was a trick played on them by people on a Japanese TV show: the presenter sat the girls down to eat a Japanese meal which they devoured – only to be told they were eating . . . grasshopper.

'We didn't find it funny,' they mused.

ITALY

B*Witched have been to Italy a couple of times, and each experience has been very different from the last. For example, one trip involved the girls flying to Milan to announce the winners at the MTV European music awards. Keavy decided to blow glitter over the envelope before she opened it – and in the process she managed to cover Lindsay with the stuff from head to toe!

Another time they went, they visited the island of Elba off the coast of Italy.

'It was like your typical Mediterranean island,' Edele told *TV Hits* magazine later. 'With all the beautiful villas, trees and wild flowers . . . it was really peaceful. I don't think I'd want to live there though. It was lovely for a holiday but if you lived there there'd be nothing to do.'

SWEDEN

The girls' first trip to Sweden turned out to be a bit 'odd', to say the least. They reckon that from the very beginning, everything seemed to go wrong. Perhaps the worst part was when they had to perform on a stage which became soaking wet because a fountain in front of it was spraying the floor. The slippery staging proved to be a little too tricky for all that Irish dancing!

FRANCE

In autumn 1997 the B*Witched girls managed to net themselves a pretty jammy trip – a visit to Disneyland near Paris. They had a fantastic time and managed to go on the Space Mountain ride six times (pretty apt considering they had a number one hit with 'Rollercoaster'!).

Unfortunately though, it was pretty nippy weather, so their lovely record company bought them Mickey Mouse puffa jackets to keep the B*Witchers warm. They still have the jackets as a great souvenir of their trip.

WHERE NEXT?

They've been spellbound by Asia, astounded by America and

enchanted by Europe. So where would our B*Witchers like to go next?

'I'd really like to go to Africa,' says Edele.

'Yeah,' agrees Sinead. 'I'd really like to go on safari and see the lions.'

'It's the only continent I haven't been to so I'd love to go, especially to South Africa,' says Lindsay. 'I've seen loads of pictures of it and it looks absolutely stunning. Cape Town, Table Mountain . . . all those kinds of places.'

'Who knows?' says Sinead. 'Our record company might launch us there next!'

The strain of travelling

What are the worst things about travelling for B*Witched?

Lindsay: 'Sometimes when we're a bit tired or homesick one of us will snap at the others. But I think everyone gets like that, no matter how well you get on.'

Sinead: 'Travelling can put a big strain on you – you really get to know someone when you spend all that time together. But I think we know the ins and outs of each other by now. We know how to read each other's moods.'

Keavy: 'We're all in the same boat so we understand what it's like.'

Edele: 'I don't think we've ever had any major fall-outs, though. I know it's boring but we really do get on very well!'

Favourite countries

Having seen so much of the world, Edele, Keavy, Sinead and Lindsay have definite ideas about their favourite places . . .

'I've always loved going back to Greece, where I was born,' says Lindsay. 'I don't get to go there as often as I'd like, which is quite sad. The best time of year to go there is the spring when all the countryside comes alive with the prettiest wild flowers. I really miss it actually.'

Sinead meanwhile prefers to stay closer to home.

'I know it might sound a bit sad,' says Sinead, 'but I really do love living in Ireland. It's my dream to have a big house by the sea there some day. I still love travelling though. I'd love to see Niagara Falls.'

Edele loves the Unites States of America.

'I just love the States,' she says. 'We went to California not long ago and did all the stuff – y'know, go to Disneyland, walk along Venice Beach. It's all just exactly as you see it on the telly. Mind you, it wasn't as hot as we thought it would be.'

As for Keavy? She can't decide which she likes best – America or Australia . . .

'We've just spent some time in New York and it was absolutely fantastic,' she told a journalist. 'It's so busy and exciting and has got loads of fantastic shops – we went totally mad there.'

As for Oz?

'I really loved it,' she smiles. 'It was so warm and sunny. It's such an amazing country, so big, and with all that amazing wildlife like kangaroos and koalas! Great!'

CHAPTER TWELVE

B*Witched Are in the House!

You know what B*Witched are like on stage, you've got a pretty good idea of what they're like on the road . . . but do you ever wonder what happens when they're off duty and doing normal, everyday things at home? Well, here's your chance to find out, as we take a look at the girls in their own natural habitat . . .

The Irish homestead

All four of the B*Witched girls are very lucky to come from fantastic family homes back in Ireland. Until she joined B*Witched, Lindsay lived with her mum, Sinead was living in flats around Dublin (but was only a short ride away from the family home she shared with her Ma, Da and brothers and sisters) – and Edele and Keavy? Well perhaps they were the luckiest.

The twins had spent all of their lives living with their parents, three sisters and brother in their family home in Donaghmede – a house which is still full of all of the mementoes they collected while growing up. It's a fantastic house! The entrance hall is done up like a grotto with a cave-like ceiling and an indoor rock pool decorated with Chinese figures. And in the back garden there's an artificial stream surrounded by plastic deer! The Lynches have all lived happily in the house for twenty or so years, and, despite the success of Shane in Boyzone and the twins in their own careers, it has always stayed the same: there are no grand displays of wealth or grandeur – and Mr and Mrs Lynch will not accept haughty behaviour! In fact, even though, for years, Shane has been followed by thousands of girls all desperate for his attention, Ma and Pa Lynch have never changed their phone number, which can be found on the Internet! So, hour after hour, the answer-phone fills up with messages from fans for Keavy, Edele or Shane.

Over to England . . .

As you can imagine, when the girls first had to move to England so that they could begin work as pop stars, it was something of a trauma. Though Sinead had lived in England before, for the rest of the girls it was their first time away from home. Like any teenagers moving away from home, they found it an amazing and exciting adventure, but it also marked a huge and scary turning point in their lives: it was the first time they had had to stand on their own two feet and fend for themselves. The girls were teenagers desperately trying to look after themselves like adults.

The girls first moved into a lovely little four-bedroom house in the village of Egham in Surrey, found for them by their management company. Immediately they realised that they would have to rely on each other for support.

'We're like four best friends who've become a second family to each other,' Sinead told a reporter at the time.

'Yeah,' agreed Edele. 'We left Ireland for England together. None of us, apart from Sinead, had been away before so we've learnt to look after each other.'

'Our parents phone all the time though,' Keavy added. 'They ask us if we're eating properly and stuff like that.'

It seemed that no matter how far the girls were away from home, their friends and family just had to turn on a TV to see what they looked like and make sure that they were eating healthily and getting enough sleep!

The girls soon got into the swing of things and managed to arrange their household like a proper family home. They learnt to take it in turns to do domestic chores (being a pop star doesn't necessarily mean that you don't have to vacuum or do the washing up!) and they quickly realised how much fun it could be hanging out at home.

'We've got a rota for the washing up and we're all really good at taking turns,' Lindsay said at the time. 'It was scary when we first moved,' she added. 'Now it's mad. The lounge is a "no-go" area; a place just to dump our coats and bags. The washing machine doesn't work and we eat a lot of takeaways.'

We bet their parents were none too pleased! Still, they

managed to maintain a semblance of cleanliness and have a huge amount of fun in the process. Not that they were living like rock stars or anything. The girls weren't exactly partying morning, noon and night – they didn't have the time or the energy!

'We go crazy,' Keavy told the *Daily Star* when a reporter asked them how they spent their evenings. 'We watch loads of films on telly and drink loads of milk!'

Rock 'n' roll!

The only problem the girls really encountered at their house in Egham was their faulty washing machine. Luckily, after 'C'est La Vie' went to number one, they celebrated by buying a new one!

London girls

At the beginning of 1999, the girls decided to move closer to the English capital – to a swish pad in Battersea in south-west London. The flat was gorgeous, with wooden floors and swanky sofas, but it was still comfy enough to be a home from home.

'It's hard to put your roots down,' Keavy told journalist Julia Kuttner when she visited the girls in their new pad. 'But this isn't a long-term base.'

The pictures of the flat showed that the girls had definitely acquired some taste in their year of living together. Hanging on the wall in their very clean living room was a fantastic arty picture which an up-and-coming artist called Rachel Deacon had done of the four B*Witched girls.

'It really has become a treasured item,' Edele said. 'If we ever move apart there'll be a squabble. We'll probably have to cut it into pieces!'

Despite their new washing machine, doing laundry in the new flat is still a bit of a headache.

'We've got a washing machine but no tumble dryer yet, so if we're in a rush and our clothes aren't dry we have to wear them as they are,' Keavy explained. 'And damp denim isn't comfortable, I can tell ya.'

We'll bet.

Months have passed since the girls moved into the Battersea pad and they're now very much at home. Their coffee table is crammed with magazines like *Smash Hits*, *Big* and *OK!* (they try to send their cuttings back home for their families to keep) and the place is also littered with chocolate wrappers – choccie being the girls' biggest vice.

'We like to bring certain chocolates over with us from Ireland,' Edele explains. 'It tastes really different – it's the flavour of home.'

The flat is also scattered with bottles of water – very handy seeing as the girls manage to drink two and a half litres of the stuff each, every day (alongside their obligatory half a pint of milk)!

As for cooking? Well, you'll be glad to hear that nowadays the girls are much more organised and are doing a heck of a lot of their own meal preparation instead of buying the nasty takeaways they used to rely on. Eating well is now a big part of B*Witched's philosophy and the girls are determined to make sure they eat the right foods and get their daily intake of vitamins and minerals. Not that they're very imaginative when it comes to their menus . . .

'When we're all at home we tend to cook the same things over and over again,' says Sinead. 'Roast chicken, Irish chicken stew, sweet and sour chicken or pasta with chicken and tomato sauce. You could say we like our chicken!'

As for who is the best cook? No one's prepared to say. But they do agree on one thing – it isn't Edele.

'Edele's the worst,' Sinead says. 'She puts salt on everything. We do tend to fall out when we cook together!'

Each of the girls has managed to add her own home comforts into their London home, as they know it's the small familiar touches which stop them from getting homesick.

As Sinead says, 'I make sure I have a few personal things with me so everywhere can feel like home. For instance, I take my white polar bear everywhere with me – I can't sleep without him. My mum bought him for me ten years ago and we never spend a night apart!'

Keavy's home comforts, meanwhile, include a pair of battered clowns which she likes because of their friendly faces.

'They're my favourite toys,' she says. 'I've started to collect them.'

It seems that life in the B*Witched family home is as comfy and friendly as anyone could dream of. So if you find yourself one night wondering what the girls are up to, know this: if they're in the country, chances are that they'll have whipped up a nice chicken meal, turned on the lamps and snuggled up on the sofa to watch an episode of their favourite TV show *Friends*.

Hmm. Sounds great. Wonder if they've got a spare room . . . ?

CHAPTER THIRTEEN

First We Take Manhattan . . .

At the beginning of 1999 the B*Witched girls had cast a spell over most of the world. Britain was totally enchanted, Europe was charmed and even as far as Australia, young music fans were bopping along to the sound of 'C'est La Vie', 'Roller-coaster' and 'To You I Belong'. The girls had managed to sprinkle their fairy dust over at least three corners of the globe – but the biggie still had to be conquered: AMERICA.

It's a dream of all British bands to 'make it in the States'. With its mammoth population and amazing media network, having a hit single there can make the difference between lasting fame and fortune and being a mediocre 'two-year' band.

Luckily for B*Witched, they already had a plan to conquer the United States. They had been signed on to support 'N Sync on their American tour.

The 'N Sync tour turned out to be the beginning of a period of intense work for the girls in the States. In fact, by

July the girls were to have spent almost all of the year on the other side of the Atlantic.

'The 'N Sync tour was grand. We had a great time,' Sinead told a journalist later. 'At first we were a bit apprehensive about touring with such a well known boy band, but the fans were really welcoming for the first gig in Minneapolis so we started to relax and enjoy it.

'The other great thing,' she said, laughing, 'was our tour bus. It had 12 bunk beds!'

The end of the 'N Sync tour proved to be just the start of another exhilarating schedule of promotion for the Irish lasses in the US. They began to court the American public, doing interviews, concerts and TV specials. A fan on the Internet reported that, over the space of two days, the girls had managed to fly in from London to New York, then on to perform in Denver – via a gig in Oklahoma! – and then to Canada that same night!

If only they could use broomsticks!

One of the highlights for the girls had to be when they made an appearance on America's favourite *Tonight* show with Jay Leno. The show has been on-air since the Sixties and was actually credited with bringing the Beatles to the US! Would history repeat itself with the B*Witched girls? New B*Witched fans in the States tuned in to watch the interview and hung on to every word our Irish ambassadors said.

Sinead admitted that she was missing Ireland like crazy. 'I miss Dublin and just bumping into people,' she said, a tad sadly. 'To be honest, the last time I was home I felt very strange and uncomfortable because my friends have got new friends and I felt a bit awkward, as though I was missing things.'

Still, life in the States was far too exciting for the girls to get glum – and anyway they had some pretty interesting work to look forward to. They weren't in the US just to do promo work – they were there to record their next album!

Producer Ray Hedges had flown out to LA to get the girls started on their next record. This way they could conquer America and actually make an album at the same time. Now the girls were interspersing their hard promotional work with fun in the studio!

So what was the new album going to be like? The *Sun* newspaper was determined to find out, so interviewed the girls in LA.

'We wanted to make a similar record to the last one, as it had our own unique style,' the girls said. 'All our singles were different though so our fans can expect to hear some more great songs on the next one.'

With a second album on the way it really did look like B*Witched were going to be a lasting influence on the pop world – or, as they said in one of their not-so-famous songs, 'We four girls are here to stay.'

While the B*Witchers laid down their album tracks (man!), their record company in the States prepared a series of tours and concerts for them.

In May the girls joined a US band called 98 Degrees and supported them on their inter-state tour. It was another chance for them to make new friends and influence people.

Their plan was definitely working. 'C'est La Vie'

managed to enter the Billboard charts at number nine, while their album managed number twelve. The magic was spreading.

The girls, meanwhile, were looking forward to a quick trip home to Ireland.

'We're going back on the 14 of May, which is my birthday,' Sinead told an American journalist. 'We're going back for nine days, and then we go to England for a few days to do some more recording on our second album. Then we're back [in the US], basically for the rest of the summer.'

While they were back in the UK, B*Witched had a bit of unfinished business to attend to. Their first single, 'C'est La Vie', had been nominated in two categories for the prestigious Ivor Novello awards. They'd been nominated for best song (musically and lyrically) and best-selling UK single. The girls weren't expecting to win. They were up against stiff competition. Not only were Edele and Keavy pitching against their brother Shane's band, Boyzone (who had been nominated for their single 'No Matter What'), they were also against Cher's number one dance hit, 'Believe'. The swanky awards ceremony took place at the Grosvenor House Hotel, London, on 27 May – and the girls left empty-handed.

'We were just honoured to have been nominated,' Edele told TV crews cheerfully – making it very clear that the girls had had a fantastic night.

Not that they cared. They arrived back in the US to discover that their album had just gone platinum (having sold one million copies) and that they had been asked to take part in a very special tour – the Nickelodeon 'All that and more' tour, with Monica, No Authority, Tatyana Ali, and 98 Degrees. The tour was already in progress, but B*Witched were signing on to tour with them from 23 July through until the middle of August.

But before that, in June, the girls had a chance to do something they will never ever forget – play to a stadium crowd of 79,000 people for the Women's World Cup soccer championships at Giants Stadium in East Rutherford, New Jersey.

By now the newspapers and music shows were catching on to the B*Witched phenomenon and MTV news excitedly reported on the girls' US stadium debut.

'Although the group's album has only been out a few months in the States and the quartet is comparatively unknown on these shores, it just celebrated its fourth consecutive number one single in the UK with "Blame It On The Weatherman",' they told US viewers.

And in an interview with the channel, Lindsay talked about how weird it was performing in the States.

'It's strange to be here and not have people recognising you and coming up to you all the time,' she said laughing. 'It's nice in a way, but it's also nice to get back to playing for a big crowd.'

She talked about the album recording, saying that they were progressing quite nicely with the new record.

'We're about half-way through, I think,' Lindsay said. 'We've been recording on the fly as well, grabbing studio time whenever we've had a few days off.'

She also revealed that the week before, while performing for a handful of radio stations on the west coast of the US, the band had flown up to Vancouver, of all places, to do even more work on the record with Ray. The new album was certainly turning out to be 'global music'!

The girls were still working hard in the States as this book went to press, and by all accounts the noise coming from across the pond seemed to be that America lurved liddle ole B*Witched.

The last we heard of them, they'd recorded a special Disney concert, were appearing on the soundtrack to the brilliant US TV show *Dawson's Creek* and had recorded a new video for 'Rollercoaster' – allegedly featuring the girls on a beach and visiting shops in a beach-side town in France. ('There's tons of dancing and the girls float above the pavement during the middle of the song,' a fan revealed on the Internet.)

It looks like B*Witched are well on their way to enchanting America, and whatever happens next for the girls, the one thing we're sure of is that with their style, enthusiasm and charm, the world is their proverbial oyster. Their success in the States has a lot to do with their charisma and determination – and maybe a little to do with the luck of the Irish . . .

CHAPTER FOURTEEN

B*Witched and their Heavenly Bodies!

Some things are just meant to be, and when you look at how naturally B*Witched have fought their way to stardom, you do begin to wonder if this is what was destined for them . . . Could it be that our B*Witchers were born to be famous and that their place in pop's history books was first written in the stars?

No doubt B*Witched would argue that the only way they made it to the top was through sheer hard work, determination and the all-important factor of treating everyone around them with respect, but, for a bit of fun, let's take a look at the girls' horoscopes to see if they could have been nudged in the right direction by fate!

There are a lot of archers around here . . .

Perhaps the weirdest thing, astrologically, about B*Witched

is that three of them share the same sun sign! Edele and Keavy are both Sagittarians (we'd expect them to be, seeing as they were born on the same day! Doh!) – but then so is Lindsay, who was born a year and three days later. This means that Edele and Keavy (born on 15 December 1979) and Lindsay (born on 18 December 1980) should share an amazing number of interests, goals and character traits.

Sinead, on the other hand, has her sun sign in Taurus. As a Taurean (born on 14 May 1978) she has her feet firmly on the ground ('I'm earthy,' she says) and so she probably provides a steadying influence on the other three.

Let's have a look in depth to see what these star signs really mean . . .

Edele, Keavy and Lindsay – the Sagittarians

Not only are these three B*Witchers Sagittarians, but they're late Sagittarians, which means that they were born in the last sector of the sun sign. People born around this time are meant to have a strong need and desire for success, plus a highly positive attitude towards everything – which sums them up to a T! (You'll hardly ever hear these three complaining, even when they're tired or have 'flu!)

Late Sagittarians have very strong willpower, unfaltering strength and unwavering determination – if they set their hearts on something they make sure that they focus on it and are never tempted to give up. Edele, Keavy and Lindsay understand that to make dreams come true, hard work needs to happen, which is probably why, from the very beginning, they shut themselves up in the Digges Lane studio and insisted that they were 'training for their dreams' – even though they had little idea at that time how easily those dreams would come true.

Perhaps the most evident thing about Sagittarians is that they have extremely strong and compelling personalities. Some astrologers reckon that archers' personalities give them 'star quality', which is why so many of them make it as film stars, politicians and singers! The main thing about their characters, however, is that they express a great joy in life – and, as we know, the girls from B*Witched reckon that what they're doing is celebrating life in a way that only they can. Their astrological types are spot-on so far!

Now here's a warning for the three girls: sometimes their constant smiling and energetic ramblings make people think that they're a bit, well, insincere. Other people are so used to having to deal with the seriousness of life and the pressures and stresses of work that they can't believe that these Irish lovelies can always be happy and up! They may wonder whether the girls are just 'turning on' their smiles to get what they want – in which case, this may rub people up the wrong way. Of course, the girls are genuine – they just have a very positive outlook on life. They know how to make the best of a situation and so – even when the worst things happen to them – they simply shrug their shoulders and meet the challenge, positive that they'll come out the other side as stronger people, having learnt another of life's lessons.

The main thing 'Del, Keaves and Linds have to look out for is wasting their energy. Sometimes their constant jumping and running around tires them out, when really they should have been conserving their energy for more important things.

They also need to become a tad more organised. They are very homely people but tend to be a bit flutter-headed and never seem to have enough time to get things done, so in the end their flat regularly looks like a bomb has hit it. (The Sagittarian's idea of cleaning up is to dump everything under a bed or in the sink to deal with later!)

Perhaps the worst trait they have is 'foot in mouth' disease, meaning that sometimes they don't think before they speak, or even if they do it comes out the wrong way. They already had a bit of trouble with this when they said a joke-naughty word on British telly (a word they didn't even realise was swearing!) and then got told off for it by the ITC!

On the whole, though, that's a small sacrifice to make for being such warm-hearted, generous and gregarious people!

Sinead – the Taurean!

You'd think it would be difficult for Sinead, being the only non-Sagittarius in B*Witched, but actually she has the perfect balance of inspiration and stability to cope with the other three girls at play.

Like the others, Sinead was born in the later half of her astrological sign, and as such she manages to be much more studious and serious than the typical Taurean. This is probably why she was such a top student and managed to earn the title Schoolgirl of the Year when she was younger!

As she herself says, she's very earthy and tends to have the amazing quality of being a dreamer while at the same time keeping a good sense of reality, and she is practical about what she can and can't achieve at a particular time. Taureans love food (which is probably why Sinead is such a great cook!) and look after money well so, at the end of the day, she will always have a comfortable home and will be able to provide for her own needs.

And when Taureans are at home they love relaxing in front of the TV and eating comfort food – and you just have to look at the chapter about B*Witched's house to see how true that is.

As a Taurean, Sinead is responsible, dutiful and persevering. She will make sure she does her work to the best of her ability and will try never to let anyone down.

Out of all of the B*Witched girls, Sinead should be the least easy to really get to know, yet when people take the trouble to break the ice and talk to her, they realise that Sinead likes to take time to develop trust and is the truest and most loyal friend a person could have.

Taureans have a certain degree of anxiety and worry in their personalities – they tend to be cautious and a little reserved. Only Sinead's closest friends could tell you whether that's true about her.

The spookiest thing about Sinead's sun sign is this: the very famous astrologer Teri King (who syndicates astrology columns throughout the world) reckons that Taureans born towards the end of their sun sign tend to find that 'in their youth their fathers threw a restricting influence over their life' – just as Sinead explained earlier! She says that Taureans tend to follow their father's example, which is why they become extremely disciplined!

Perhaps the best thing about Taureans, though, is that they are terribly reliable – and that is very evident when it comes to their friendships. Those lucky B*Witched girls!

Let's go a bit animal crackers . . .

Because three of the B*Witched girls share the same star sign, it might be worth having a look at a different sort of astrology – Chinese horoscopes. The Chinese sages reckon that everyone is born in the year of an animal – be it rat, pig, dragon or whatever – and that looking at the year someone is born in tells you what kind of person they are.

Edele and Keavy were born in the year of the Goat, Lindsay was born in the year of the Monkey, and Sinead was born in the year of the Horse.

EDELE AND KEAVY - GOAT GIRLS!

As Goats, Edele and Keavy have particularly considerate and caring natures. They are very loyal to family and friends and are invariably well liked. Goat people are reliable and conscientious in work but find it difficult to save and never like to deprive themselves of luxuries. (So we guess the twins will be splashing out on lots of Irish choccies when their royalties come in!)

Goat girls usually get pleasure following the activities of various members of their families (we kid you not!) so it's not surprising then that the twins followed their big bruv into the music industry!

LINDSAY - MONKEYING AROUND!

Lindsay is a Monkey, which means she's very strong-willed and sets about everything she does with steely determination. She is ambitious, wise and confident and relishes hard work. Apparently, Monkeys are very astute when it comes to money matters so, like Sinead, Lindsay will probably always have a nest egg hidden away somewhere. Finally, despite having an independent nature and needing some time on her own, she also enjoys attending parties and is very warm and caring towards loved ones.

SINEAD - THE GALLOPING GOURMET!

In Chinese astrology, Sinead is a Horse, which means that she is terribly considerate and caring. Horses are a little more cautious than some other types, but are very wise, perceptive and extremely capable. As a Horse, Sinead can be a bit indecisive at times, but she has great business know-how and could be the member of B*Witched who worries most about her future and where she's heading to. Generally though, she should have a quiet, friendly nature and should be well thought of by her family and friends.

How they get on . . .

According to Chinese Astrology, Edele and Keavy should get on well because Goats get on well with other Goats and have a lot of objectives and ambitions in common. Lindsay and the twins should get on like a house on fire too, because Monkeys and Goats have a mutual respect and understanding for each other (apparently!). The twins and Sinead should be the best of friends because Horses and Goats are very compatible and make excellent friendships. In fact, the only wee problem the girls should have is between Lindsay and Sinead, because Monkeys and Horses sometimes have a clash of personalities. We're sure, though, that with their shared experience and deep love for each other, they are firm friends anyway!

Chinese forecasts for the year 2000, the year of the Dragon

SINEAD

This is an important year for Horses and their careers, it seems. For Sinead it is a time to move forward and build on her past successes. Early on in the year, she has to concentrate on doing what she already does well, so just keep on dancing and singing, Sinead! The best bit of news for Miss O'Carroll is that at some point in 2000 she will receive a tip or some good advice which will help her gallop to unimaginable success!

EDELE AND KEAVY

Friendships which Goats make in the year 2000 will play an important part in their futures. At work this year, they need to proceed with care and stay aware of what is happening around them. It's an excellent time to take stock of what they have already achieved and spend time deciding how they would like their careers to develop. If they fancy doing some new training – learning more about songwriting, say, or taking up playing a new insttrument – the year 2000 will give them the best opportunity.

LINDSAY

It's time for Monkeys to move forward, Lindsay, so the year 2000 will be the year for you to make even more of your talents and abilities. Lindsay should look for opportunities and openings to help the band make it even bigger than they've managed already. Lindsay's Chinese chart says that she will do less travelling – and have better romance prospects. Looks like love is on the cards for you, Linds!

Sun sign predictions for the girls in the year 2000

Make of this what you will!

Pluto passes through Sagittarius this year which means 'transformation' – or personal change – for our three Sagittarian B*Witchers. They may become more serious and a little muddle-headed and dreamy and suffer from changes of opinion. People will be a little confused at our B*Witched girls because usually Sagittarians are easy to read. Meanwhile, Jupiter, the planet of good fortune, will be in the opposite sign of Gemini come July. It will throw luck over all partnership affairs!

As for Sinead? Well, Taureans may find it difficult to speak their minds in the year 2000. Uranus will pass through Sinead's chart and, as it's the planet of chaos she can expect quite a few surprises. This is good as it will stop her from sticking to what she knows best and shake her into action. However, Saturn will be in her sign all year long, so she'll have brilliant focus and concentration!

CHAPTER FIFTEEN

Magic Up your Life!

Okay. It's time to get serious for a bit! When you watch B*Witched on TV and read their interviews you probably spend an awful lot of time wishing that you could be them! Part of you probably wants to be famous, another part wants to wear gorgeous clothes and look like them and an iddy bit of you wishes that you could be as cool and together as Edele, Keavy, Sinead and Linds.

Unfortunately, you aren't B*Witched. You probably get grumpy when you have to go to school and do geography (instead of swanning about a TV studio doing pop interviews), a little down when you look in the mirror (it's perfectly natural, we all have our bad days!), and a tad depressed when you realise that the most exotic place you're going to visit this year is the tropical fruit counter at your local supermarket.

Well, here's the good news: while you might not be able to be B*Witched, you can be like B*Witched. Each of our four B*Witchers is just like you; they all had their down moments when they were growing up! The secret to their success, however, is their positive attitude. Our girls have managed to achieve their brilliant lives by being POSITIVE! Want to be like them? It's easy when you know how! Here's how to get the B*Witched cool-life philosophy!

1) REMEMBER THAT TRUE FRIENDS ARE FOREVER!

One of the reasons that the girls have such a great life is because they know that in their darkest moments they have the support of their other three B*Witchers! They aren't the kind of girls to bitch and backstab their mates. True friends, like Lindsay, Sinead, Keavy and Edele, look out for each other. They tell each other when they're looking great, they appreciate the finer points of each other's personalities and they help each other to achieve what they want. What's more, the girls would never sacrifice their friendships for boys, 'cause at the end of the day they know that when their relationships end their mates are always there for them!

Try spreading the 'friends' philosophy throughout your life. Make sure you appreciate your mates. Make sure that you're being the best friend you can be. Ask them how they are, consider their feelings and be sure to be there for them when they're a little down. If you become a good mate, you'll find you get so much love back you'll never feel lonely!

2) MAKE THE MOST OF YOURSELF!

So you think life is a disaster when you look in the mirror and see you've got spots or a wonky nose or a bad hairdo? Get real! All four of our B*Witched girls look gorgeous most of the time, yet none of them are supermodel gorgeous like Natalie Imbruglia or Kate Moss! All the girls have their little quirks (take Edele's scar, for instance) but they know that it's their imperfections that make them so beautiful. The secret to looking and feeling great B*Witched-style is simply to make the most of what you've got! So long as you're clean, take pride in your appearance and smile lots, you will always be attractive! Make a note of your favourite features and concentrate on them when you're getting ready to go out. And here's a little magical spell to make sure you're feeling at your best: if you look at yourself in the mirror before you leave the house and say, 'I'm gorgeous, I'm gorgeous, I'm gorgeous, and my beauty shines from within,' you'll find that you emanate a positive vibe all day!

3) NEVER BE NEGATIVE

Our B*Witched girls know that happiness is in the head! In other words, if you convince yourself that life is great then it will be great. On the other hand, if you're negative about life and think that you're stupid, ugly and boring, then the chances are that you'll come across that way to other people! If you want to be like B*Witched, don't ever think a negative thought. If you find yourself giving yourself a hard time about something (for example, if you're feeling low because you feel dowdy and dull), learn to stop yourself immediately! Tell your brain to get a grip, and shove the bad thoughts straight from your mind (you can imagine putting the nasty thoughts into a dustbin and banging the lid on them!). Then concentrate on being positive for the rest of the day. If you're positive, other people will be positive towards you!

4) BELIEVE ANYTHING IS POSSIBLE

Becoming a pop star is one of the hardest things in the world

– some would say it is nearly impossible to achieve. There are so many people out there trying to make it in the music industry that it would be easy to say, 'What's the use? It'll never happen!' and then give up.

Luckily for us, B*Witched refused to have that attitude. They knew that nothing was impossible, no matter how tricky or unlikely, so they put their minds to realising their dreams . . . and did it! It's fair enough to err on the safe side, and make sure you have alternatives if your dreams don't quite take shape (look at Lindsay – she had her place at college to fall back on if B*Witched didn't work out). However, having a safety net is just an insurance policy. If you want to achieve something, imagine it in your mind's eye and then don't let anything stop you from achieving it. It may take some time, but nothing is impossible.

5) DON'T LET OTHER PEOPLE'S BAD VIBES GET YOU DOWN

It's an unfortunate fact that as you go through life you'll come across negative people who try to bring you down. As we've seen, B*Witched have had their fair share of this with the scurrilous hacks of the tabloid press. Sometimes, when you become successful at something, other people become jealous and bitter – often because they're wondering whether they could have achieved something more with their lives if they'd only tried a bit harder, like you. Jealous people can say all sorts of hurtful things. In the beginning, some people tried to insinuate that B*Witched had only become successful because the twins' brother was Shane from Boyzone! Other successful pop stars have come in for ribbing too. Take Geri

Haliwell, who was called fat and ugly when it's obvious to anyone with half a brain that she's gorgeous. The trick to dealing with negative criticism like this is to take it as a compliment! Seriously!

If so-called friends start bitching about you behind your back, or making hurtful comments to you about your attitude, looks or dreams, laugh it off and feel pleased. They're only trying to bring you down because they're jealous. Take a leaf from B*Witched's book and use negative criticism to spur you on to even dizzier heights. Success is the best revenge!

6) REMEMBER, BLOOD IS THICKER THAN WATER

It's easy to take your family for granted, especially when you have to spend your mornings fighting to use the bathroom and your evenings arguing with your mum and dad about what time you have to be home. Unfortunately, all too often the silly day-to-day tiffs of family life can leave you wishing that you lived alone, far away from the family home. Don't fall into this trap! All the B*Witched girls have learnt quickly that their families are their safe havens. When things get too much for them, and they need a friendly ear or a shoulder to cry on, our girls always know that their brothers, sisters, mums and dads will be there to support them. Get the B*Witched attitude and treat your family with respect. You never know when you'll need them!

7) TREAT EVERY DAY AS A CHANCE TO DO SOMETHING NEW!

As the girls often say, life is for living, so live it! Don't let yourself fall into a rut in which you do the same boring thing day in, day out. To get the B*Witched attitude to life, you need to value every waking second. When you wake up every morning, ask yourself, 'If this was the last day in my life, what would I like to do?' And then do it! Obviously this doesn't give you the excuse to walk into school and pour custard over your most hated teacher! (Nice try . . .) And if you want to be a NASA astronaut, you may find it takes a little more than a day to achieve it! But set yourself goals. If you know you want to do something, don't just dream about it and wish your life away. Put you dreams into practice! Remember, if B*Witched hadn't got their jobs (in shops and garages and theatres) they wouldn't have had the money to book rehearsal time in the Digges Lane dance studio. And if they hadn't booked time in the dance studio, they would never have got their act together. And if they hadn't got their act together, they never would have impressed the people from the RTE TV station who asked them to appear on their show . . . Get the picture? Don't just dream it, do it!

8) LOOK AFTER YOURSELF!

It's difficult to make the most of your life if you're always tired and run down. Energy is one of the keys to B*Witched's success. They've got it in bucket loads, as anyone who has ever met them will tell you – they're always jumping and dancing around. To make sure you have the same amount of energy, look after yourself. Eat right, drink lots of water (you have to stay hydrated!) and get plenty of sleep. And remember what the girls said in a previous chapter about looking gorgeous: you don't need a gym to exercise! A run in the park, a dance at the disco or simply bouncing around in your day-to-day life will keep your body fit and your energy levels high!

9) YOU DON'T HAVE TO BE HARD TO BE COOL!

When you're in your teens you'll often find that some of the 'coolest' people in your circle seem to be the sultry, hipper-than-thou ones. You know the type – they walk around with miserable faces, making cynical quips at everything and making out like the only way to be cool is to be unenthusiastic and laid-back. They seem to become popular by frightening everyone – it's almost as if people become their mates because they're frightened that they'll get picked on if they don't. Dump that attitude! The B*Witched girls prove that you can be much cooler by being cheerful and nice to people. In the past B*Witched have been accused of being squeaky clean, but so what? There's nothing wrong with being squeaky clean. If anything, it's great to be squeaky clean because you have nothing to hide and you can live with yourself knowing that you're a nice person. So don't be afraid to be uncool. It's probably the coolest thing you can do!

10) RESPECT OTHERS!

The final bit of the B*Witched attitude is to treat others with respect. It would have been all too easy for our heroines to develop a bad attitude when they became famous, but because of the way they've been brought up they would never think they were better than anyone. It doesn't matter what people do – whether they're milkmen, teachers, shop assistants or pop stars – we are all equal under the skin. So treat people with respect and they'll afford you the same courtesy.

Now, here's a chance for you to record your thoughts and feelings about your favourite ever pop band!

My favourite B*Witched song is . . . because . . .

Why I love B*Witched . . .

If I was a member of B*Witched I'd like to be. . . because . . .

My favourite piece of B*Witched advice is . . .

And remember, the best piece of magic you can have in your life is positivity! Try and be the best person you can and you'll be amazed at just how enchanting your life can be!

CHAPTER SIXTEEN

Thirty Things You Never Knew about B*Witched . . .

So you reckon you know everything there is to know about B*Witched, do you? Don't be so sure! Before you even attempt our tricky quiz in the next pages, swot up with this spellbinding info because we reckon these are thirty things you do not know about Lindsay, Keavy, Edele and Sinead!

1) Edele was slagged off at school for having small boobies. 'They called me titch,' she says now. 'I don't really care these days – we're all different.'

2) Lindsay once took the denim thing a bit too far – by wearing it to a wedding. 'It was quite embarrassing,' she says. 'I was moving at the time and had forgotten to pack my wedding outfit.' Ouch.

3) Lindsay is very philosophical about life: 'Just try and look for the good in every situation and tell yourself you'll always get through it however bad it seems.'

4) The last white Christmas Keavy remembers happened when she was six. 'We had a van,' she explains, 'and when the roads were icy our dad used to attach tyres, rocking horses and bits of cardboard to the back. Then we'd sit on them and go flying around the roads.'

5) Keavy once told a pop journalist that love was like . . . 'a river that drowns the tender reed. You can love someone but also be in love with someone.' Wise woman, she talk cobblers . . .

6) Sinead reckons that the only way to make yourself happy . . . is to do exactly that: make yourself happy! 'At the end of the day, you have to make yourself happy otherwise you become too dependent on other people,' she says.

7) Keavy always loses her handbag when she's out. She's usually so busy dancing that she forgets where she's left it and consequently she's had her wallet nicked lots of times.

8) The naughtiest thing Lindsay can remember doing when she was younger is telling her parents she was staying at a friend's house when she was really out partying. That's two weeks' grounding for you, Linds . . .

9) The last thing Lindsay takes off at night . . . is her watch.

Apparently it ticks very loudly and she can't sleep with it 'cause it keeps her awake.

10) Lindsay is a bit of a sop when it comes to watching sloppy films. 'I cry very easily,' she admits. 'I was sobbing and shaking so much when I went to see *Titanic* that the whole cinema was staring.' The shame of it!

11) Keavy once nicked a towel from a hotel the band were staying in. 'We'd ruined it with our hair dye,' she says, pleading innocence, 'and we were too embarrassed to give it back.' Tell that to the judge, Lynch.

12) When Lindsay was ten she managed to save a litter of kittens from drowning.

13) Edele once told a journalist that she's always had a crazy desire to jump out of a plane without a parachute. Easy there, tiger . . .

14) When Edele was at school her favourite subject was metalwork. She has used this extraordinary talent to make bracelets out of forks (as you do).

15) Scurrilous rumour has it that, back home in Ireland, Edele and Keavy have a couple of ducks as pets, called Jack and Jill – and one of them hates water. They really are odd, those girls . . .

16) The Lynch girls also have rather more acceptable pets –

they're the proud owners of a school of tropical fish!

17) Lindsay is a dab hand with the old needle and thread and managed to whip up a dress for Keavy to wear for her college graduation. Just call her Lindsay-Paul Gaultier (or something).

18) Edele is petrified of spiders and hates them to the point of violence. 'I'd only ever hit one of the other girls if they had a spider in their hair,' she says. Now that's what we call a phobia.

19) Edele really hates her feet, even though they look quite tiny to us. 'They're much too big,' she says jokingly. All the better to dance on, my dear.

20) Lindsay can do a very realistic (and ultimately, scary) impression of a fire alarm.

21) One of B*Witched's fans once adopted a bush-baby for the girls as an unusual but very cute Christmas present.

22) Edele once had a pretty bad experience with a boy. She closed her eyes to kiss him – so she didn't realise when she went in for the 'peck' that he had actually turned his cheek. The rotter!

23) Keavy is still good friends with her former kick-boxing instructor, Martin.

24) The girls wrote 'To You I Belong' as a tribute to their mums and dads. What great girls . . .

25) In Japan, the B*Witched girls have been turned into (wait for it) cartoon characters on their promotional stickers. That's what we call a sticky situation!

26) Lindsay has three dogs called Snoopy, Huskey and Leah. She also has two cats called Cheeky and Chubby.

27) When she was younger, Keavy once went into McDonalds in Dublin dressed in a wetsuit! She and her friend Mark had been out on her dad's boat on the river Liffey, which runs through the city centre. They realised that they were hungry, stopped the boat and climbed up the steps to the restaurant where they purchased their Big Macs and left. (Apparently the staff had to mop up after them!)

28) Lindsay is fascinated by all things spooky and ghostlike, and is obsessed with the *X-Files*. 'I've never seen a ghost,' she smiles. 'But just because I've not experienced one doesn't mean they don't exist.' No one's going to argue with that!

29) The girls have been speaking in ickle baby talk ever since they first arrived in England. They have a made-up baby language that they speak to each other – and tend to shock poor old-fogey journalists by answering their questions twice – once in English and the second time in their baby gaga.

30) Lindsay once got thrown out of a maths class for flinging

half a Mars Bar across a classroom. She was trying to get the choccie to her mate on the other side of the class – unfortunately the Mars Bar missed her mate, flew right past her head, and hit the classroom window with a very loud 'thwack'. Teacher was not amused!

CHAPTER SEVENTEEN

How B*Witched are you?

By now you should be an expert in all things B*Witching! Having perused the pages of this book, you probably know more about B*Witched than they do . . . or do you?!!!

It's testing time!

Think you can pit your wits against the mother of all quizzes and prove to yourself just how B*Witching you are? Or are you scared that when push comes to shove you're just a fair-weather fan?

Be brave! Run through the twenty-five questions below and use a pencil to circle one correct answer for each. Think carefully, now, because there are some trick questions hidden below! Once you've finished, check your answers and face your fate. If you've been paying attention you've got nothing to worry about!

1) When B*Witched played in the Abba supergroup band at the Brit awards, which was the only member of the band not

to wear a blue wig?

a) Sinead

b) Keavy

c) Lindsay

d) Edele

2) Which of these names did B*Witched not try out before settling on their present monicker?

a) D'Zire

b) Sassy

c) Dublin Express

d) Sister

3) What kind of men does Edele like?

a) Irish ones!

b) She doesn't care so long as they treat her well

c) Scruffy dirty ones (so long as their socks are clean)

d) Any that look like Mel Gibson

4) Why did Lindsay once go to a wedding wearing denim?

a) She was trying out the new B*Witched style

b) She asked her stylist to get her an outfit for a special occasion and he thought she was going to a pop star party

c) She was moving at the time and had forgotten to pack a wedding outfit

d) She doesn't feel comfortable in girly clothes

5) Which of the following comments did Keavy give to a pop magazine about love?

a) Love is like a river that drowns the tender reed

b) Love is a many splendoured thing

c) Love makes the world go round

d) Love, do you fancy making me a cuppa

6) What happened when Edele accidentally touched a bread roll by mistake on a flight?

a) She ate it because she felt that she had spread germs on it

b) She picked it up and threw it at Lindsay

c) She put it in her bag and gave it to Sinead later

d) The air steward was really rude to her about the 'incident' so she gave him a good telling off

7) How many children does Sinead intend to have?

a) Three

b) Four

c) Two, maximum

d) Only one

8) What does Lindsay do to her hair when she's not working?

a) Takes it off and puts it in the bed side cabinet

b) Ties it in a pony tail

c) Wears hats or puts gel on it

d) Talks to it to make it grow

9) How many sisters does Keavy have?

a) Four

b) Five

c) Two

d) Three

10) Which of the following dishes are B*Witched not likely to eat at home?

a) Seafood

b) Tagliatelle carbonara

c) Chicken pasta

d) Chicken stew

11) How does Sinead flirt with boys (if she can be bothered)?

a) She makes lots of eye contact and gets very chatty

b) She says, 'D'you know who I am?'

c) She gets Keavy to flirt with them for her

d) She casts a spell on them

12) Which of the following phobias does Keavy suffer from?

a) She hates her mobile phone ringing

b) She hates chocolate

c) She's scared of the dark

d) She has nightmares about snakes

13) Why is Lindsay B*Witched's patron saint of animals?

a) Because she owns more pets that any other member

b) Because she saved a litter of kittens from drowning when she was just ten years old

c) Because she works part time in an animal sanctuary

d) Because she can talk to animals

14) How many stitches did Edele have to have when she hurt her nose as a tot?

a) Twelve

b) Seven

c) Eighteen

d) Nineteen

15) What does the tattoo on Keavy's left shoulder signify?

a) Luck

b) Hope

c) Happiness

d) Peace

16) What kind of car does Sinead have?

a) A red Fiesta

b) A Mercedes Benz

c) A Mini

d) She doesn't – she hasn't passed her driving test yet

17) Why has Keavy got a wonky finger?

a) She hurt it in the same incident in which Edele got the scar on her nose

b) Shane ran his skateboard over it when they were little

c) She bent it during the filming of 'Rollercoaster'

d) Edele shut it in a car door when they were little

18) What is the last thing Lindsay takes off before she goes to bed at night?

a) Her earrings

b) Her socks

c) Her watch

d) Her lucky ring

19) Roughly how many pairs of jeans did Keavy own at the

last count?

a) At least fifteen pairs

b) Ten pairs

c) More than twenty pairs

d) Five pairs

20) Why are Edele and Keavy goat girls?

a) They have two goats at home called Eric and Edna

b) They're always acting the goat

c) In Chinese astrology, they're born in the year of the Goat

d) They're not – they're called duck girls cause they own two
ducks

21) Which of the following is Edele a dab hand at making?

a) Carpets and rugs

b) Pottery vases

c) Belgian chocolates

d) Bracelets out for forks

22) Which band did B*Witched first tour the United States
with?

a) Boyzone

b) 911

c) 'N Sync

d) The Backstreet Boys

23) Why are Lindsay's eyes a bit spooky?

a) Because they change colour

b) Because she can turn them upside down

c) Because she can go for thirty seconds without blinking

d) Because every now and then she sees things in black and white

24) Which of the B*Witched girls once appeared in a holiday camp calendar, photographed waving from a train?
a) Keavy
b) Sinead
c) Edele
d) Lindsay

25) Why does Sinead have magical fingers?
a) She's the best in B*Witched at sprinkling fairy dust
b) She gives a great massage
c) She's very good at tinkling the ivories (i.e. playing the piano)
d) She paints her nails in magical styles

How did you score?

Reckon you've got what it takes to be a B*Witched super-fan then? Check your answers against the scorecard below. Score ten points for each correct answer!

Answers
1) a) Sinead wore a long blonde wig!
2) c)
3) c) Believe it or not! Although you score five points for saying b), as all the B*Witched girls want boys who treat them well!

4) c) The plonker!

5) a) And, no, we don't have an idea what it means either but, y'know, it's very poetic. And stuff.

6) d) 'He was really sorry at the end of it!' Edele says now!

7) c) She says she'll have one or two, but if you put d) you score five points, because Sinead reckons that if the first one hurts her too much she won't be having any more!

8) c) She reckons when she's not working she doesn't care what it looks like.

9) a) Edele (doh!), Naomi, Tara and Alison.

10 b) Sinead loves it but the other girls hate it. They all love chicken and Edele especially likes seafood!

11) a) She would never make a big thing about being a pop star though, because she wants a potential boyfriend to love her for the person she is, not for what she does.

12 c) So you're not alone!

13) b) If you put a), score five points though because she does have a lot of pets – just not as many as Keavy and Edele!

14) c) Eighteen stitches! Crikey! Good job the nurse had done her sewing homework!

15) c) Which is quite apt as Keavy has happiness in bundles!

16) d) Sinead did start taking lessons once but she gave them up because she was too frightened!

17) d) Although we must stress that Edele didn't do it on purpose.

18) c) Lindsay takes her watch off every night because she can't sleep with it on – it has an incredibly loud tick that keeps her awake.

19) a) She owns at least fifteen pairs, but if you answered c) score five points because we reckon that by the end of the year

she'll have doubled her quota!

20) c) But if you put d) score five points because they do own two ducks!

21) d) Edele loved metalwork at school and used her talents to make trendy jewellery!

22) c) Although they did tour with 911 in Britain and did one of their first ever gigs supporting Boyzone!

23) a) Her peepers mysteriously change colour from green to orange to brown depending on what mood she's in.

24) a) Even when she was a tot, Keavy had star quality!

25) b) All the girls want her to give them back rubs on tour. However, if you chose c) have five points, as Sinead learnt to play the piano when she was a wee thing.

The Results!

IF YOU SCORED 0-90 ...

Blame it on the weatherman!

Well you've got to blame it on somebody, haven't you? Are you seriously telling us that you've read this book from cover to cover and that you still couldn't get more then ten questions right? Oh do B*have!

We'd put this low score down to a temporary lapse of memory. You've obviously been doing so much Irish dancing recently that you've jiggled your brain a bit too much and it's not working properly. Never mind. Give yourself a day off today, cut down on the Irish jigging, and have another shot at the quiz tomorrow. We reckon you'll get full marks! In the meantime, if you want to B*Witch up your life a little more, listen to the girls' album and take on board their enchanting message: Life is for living so make the most of it!

IF YOU SCORED 100-190 . . .

To them you belong!

Not bad at all! Your knowledge of Sinead, Keavy, Edele and Lindsay is quite B*Witching. You know pretty much everything there is to know about the girls and can truly call yourself a B*Witched fan. There is a wee bit of room for improvement – you could probably do with polishing up on a little more trivia. But lets face it, there's more to do in life than know Sinead's shoe size and the length of Keavy's right arm! We reckon you've got the balance just right – you know a lot about B*Witched but you're not so obsessed that you don't have a life of your own. Good work there, reader! Now, go and sprinkle some of your amazing fun-loving, positive fairy dust on your family and friends.

IF YOU SCORED 200-250 . . .

C'est La Vie!

Mama mia! Have you been putting fairy dust in your tea instead of sugar? You're one of B*Witched's biggest fans, in fact – hang on a sec – you're one of the Lynch family, aren't you? Ha! You can't fool us, Shane! We know you're out there.

If you're not one of Edele and Keavy's relatives we're extremely impressed by the extent of your pop trivia. You know pretty much everything there is to know about the girls (possibly more!) and we can only suggest that you join the band as their secret fifth member, immediately. Just a word of caution though: there is such a thing as overdoing it! We know you love B*Witched, but make sure you're spending time enjoying your own life as well! B*Witched would be delighted to know how much you care about them, but they want you to have your own life too – not just live through them! Go out there and cast yourself a spell to live a magical, B*Witching life!

CHAPTER EIGHTEEN

Into the Futures . . .

B*Witched must be absolutely stunned at everything they've managed to achieve over the last few years. With their sheer hard work and determination, they've managed to conquer most of the world with their fantastic pop tunes and positive attitude, in less time than it takes to say abracadabra! (Okay, well not quite.)

Their story has been a rollercoaster ride that never comes down – and the best part of it is that the ride is still rolling! The band still has so much to achieve . . .

Towards the end of 1999, B*Witched were ready for one of the most exciting periods of their career. Their first British tour was due to kick off in November, they were planning to release a single just before it, and they had a new album in the wings just waiting to be unleashed on an expectant world!

Add to that the fact that their debut album is still continuing to sell by the warehouse load, in places as far away as Singapore and Australia, and it's easy to see why B*Witched are well on their way to becoming the most successful female group of all time.

The main thing for the girls, however, is that they

continue to make *us* happy! As Sinead told a magazine recently:

'We achieved so many things last year, we've made a lot of people happy, which is the most important thing for us. It's so lovely seeing our fans looking up at us and smiling. That is what we want to continue doing next year.'

Well, girls, our cheesy grins are at the ready . . . !